Dear Reader,

This book is about the life of psychic and healing abilities mankind. His name is Michael McGuire, known to one all as 'Mick' or 'The Healerman.' Some of the stories that he tells you will understand and others will be beyond your comprehension. Much is written about the gifted psychics that work for us but much less is said about the mediumship of healing. Healing is a gift that is born into each and every one of us and yet it is rarely spoken about in the media.

Many years ago Mick trained the now famous Rosemary Altea as a psychic and a medium. He works with the spiritual realms and is guided by the late Harry Edwards and his powerful Indian guide, Red Feather. If any of you have read Rosemary's book, 'The Eagle and the Rose,' there is a chapter in it where she speaks of 'The Healerman.' Mick McGuire is that man.

So often in life it is the ordinary man who is doing miraculous work behind the scenes. Mick's story has never been told and it will bring hope to many, his successes range from bad backs to cancer and the book holds the testimonies of his patients; some who have now passed over to the spirit world.

Healing works on every part of the body, mental, emotional and physical, but most of all on the soul. This is so very important as the material body is left behind when we pass over to the other side but the soul is eternal and a soul will never forget that it has been healed. Healing does not depend upon race or religion, it is a gift to all of God's children; it is for every living thing.

This book is about Mick's journey of teaching, working with the spirit doctors and healers. I hope that it will inspire all of you to use your own healing gifts and to use God's healing gift for the good of all. You were meant to use it; it is part of the skills that you were born with. So, my dear friends, whether you are fortunate enough to have good health or are suffering at the moment, please keep an open mind, have faith and read on.

Healerman 1

Mick McGuire

HEALERMAN 1

Library of Congress Catalogue No.2007021489

First Published in the UK by
Paul Mould Publishing
15 Standish Grove, Boston, Lincolnshire PE21 9EA
www.GetPublished.com
In association with
Empire Publishing Service
P.O. Box 1344, Studio City, CA 91614-0344
www.ppeps.com

A CIP Catalogue record for this book is available either from the British Library or, as below, from the US Library of Congress.

Simultaneously published in
Australia, Canada, Germany, UK, USA

Printed in Great Britain

First Printing 2007

Library of Congress Cataloging-in-Publication Data
Healerman 1 / by Mick McGuire
p. cm.
ISBN-13: 978-1-58690-062-5
1. McGuire, Mick. 2. Healers-Great Britain-Biography. 3. Guides (Spiritualism) I. Title.
RZ408.M44 2007
615.8'52092-dc22
[B]
2007021489

US 13 ISBN 978-1-58690-062-5
UK 13 ISBN 978-1-904959-54-0

Contents

The Early Years

I was born on the 4th August 1946, in a beautiful village, called Mile Oak, in Tamworth, Staffordshire, which is in the midlands area of England. Ours was quite a large family; consisting of my elder brother Jim, who was named after my father, and later on the family was completed when my mother adopted three more children, a boy and a girl and then later, in 1956, my sister Janice. Although they were adopted, they were very much my real brother and sisters, as they came to us from a very young age.

Looking back on my early childhood, it was a wonderful time. We lived in a nice semi-detached house, with a huge, typically English garden that had a fine array of fruit trees. Each day it was either apple pie or gooseberry crumble for pudding. At the bottom was a sand pit containing our buckets and spades. The garden backed on to the garden of my paternal grandparents and I would climb over the fence and run past the chicken pen, to go to grandma's for tea. I always felt loved and wanted by the people in that house. Grandma would make me an omelette with the fresh eggs that had been collected that morning. I would be allowed to sit in the front room and watch the television. This was wonderful, as we did not have a television at my house.

I remember that all the televisions had a big magnifying glass in front of the screen, as the screens were so small in those days. There was not any day-time television as there is today; the programmes did not begin until teatime. My grandfather was a coal miner, so he would be at work most of the time and in the summer grandma would invite all of my cousins to come round and we would have a party. These were the happiest of times.

Jip, the Jack Russell, was also very much a part of our family and one summer she gave birth to a litter of gorgeous, brown-eyed puppies. We were even allowed to see them being born and spent days chasing them around the garden, running and climbing the trees. The days were full of laughter and life could not have been any better. I loved Jip and those puppies. One summer's morning however, this was all to quickly change.

The postman was on his daily delivery round and started to make his way up the path. Jip's puppies were around and Jip, being the ever-protective mother, attacked and bit the postman. She was really only using her natural instincts and defending her precious babies, because after all he was on her territory. My mother however, did not see it this way and the events that followed were too horrendous for words. She ordered Jip and the puppies to be killed. In those days it was always the butcher who did this dreadful task. That Friday night all the children were bathed and sat around the kitchen table for supper. We knew that the butcher was coming at six o'clock, coming to kill our beloved dogs. I could hear Jip and her puppies crying outside the kitchen door, waiting to come in as they normally did. I sat there shaking with terror and sobbing my heart out. We had been with Jip the dog, from being babies ourselves and had become bonded with her new puppies. I felt such despair, but I was too young and powerless to be able to do anything about it. The butcher came and he brought with him his huge hammer. He bludgeoned Jip and her puppies to death. My heart was broken at this act of intense cruelty. I felt that day that my childhood had ended. I actually had hypnotherapy many years later, to try to forgive my mother for killing my best friends. However my love for animals and the healing of them has never ceased.

Life never seemed to be the same after that day and yet another trauma was to follow. We were to move out of our home, leaving behind my grandparents, all our aunts and uncles and of course all our friends. We were moving out of our lovely village to a terraced house in a mining village in South Yorkshire. I was by this time five years old, and I have never felt so lonely in all of my life. It was a very different environment from the one that I had been used to. It was grey and harsh and had no greenery. There was a lot of poverty around and the kids there were extremely tough. I was the 'new Brummie kid' in the playground, with the funny accent and took many a beating because of this. I soon learned to fight though, the Yorkshire kids were tough, but so was Mick McGuire. My maternal grandparents lived in this area, which was the reason for the family coming here but they very much favoured my older brother and didn't really want much to do with me or my adoptive brother and sister. I remember them taking Jim to Spain and buying him lots of presents and gifts; even a camera that cost a hundred pounds. I didn't want gifts though. I wanted a cuddle from the gran and grandad that I had left behind. My heart ached for them, I did not realise that I would not see them for many years to come.

We were all christened into the Catholic Church when we were born, but my mother had a fall-out with the priest, and sent us to the Baptist School in Doncaster. I remember my mother falling ill and I sat and prayed at her bedside, telling God that if she got better I would never be naughty again and I would do anything that he asked me. Of course when she was well again, I went back to my usual ways, just a normal little lad. She then sent us to the church of Saint Philip and Saint James, in Doncaster, where I was later confirmed. I have always been a performer and even at such a young age I had a love of singing. I was in the Church choir and of course I stood there with the little white ruffle around my neck, a rogue in angel's robes. I was picked to sing solo in Sheffield Cathedral. I had 'been out' with half of all the lovely girls in Bentley. I started off with the girl-next-door, and gradually worked my way down the street, not bad for a lad of ten years.

I had to work quite hard as a young boy, as a lot of the kids in Yorkshire did in those times. Money was extremely scarce in all families and at the age of eleven years, I was the proud owner of three jobs. I had a morning paper round, which I did for seven mornings a week. This paid me the princely sum of twelve shillings and sixpence, which is about 62p in present day money. I was also a delivery boy for the Thrift grocery store and had a bike with a basket on the front and I delivered groceries on Tuesday, Thursday, Friday and Saturday, and also during lunchtime at school. For this I was paid fifteen shillings or 75p. My final job of the week was at Jackson's pig farm. I mucked out the pigs each night until 9.00 p.m. and worked there on Saturday and Sunday afternoons. This paid me thirty shillings or £1.50. This gave me no time for mischief and all my efforts finally came to fruition when I purchased my very own bike.

The only recollection that I have of Spirit as a child was that there were always 'people' in my room, but I thought that this was quite normal. I always told my parents about them but they dismissed it as childhood fantasy. I had vivid, recurring dreams, of being chased by buffaloes. I also remember being visited by two beautiful angels that were so large their heads went right through the roof of my bedroom. They gave off the most brilliant light, which lit up every bit of the room, I didn't know at that time what a large part of my life Spirit was to be.

On leaving school at fifteen, I went back to work on the farm for a few months. I then got a job as a trainee waiter at the Crown Hotel in Bawtry. It was the old stagecoach house, where allegedly, Dick Turpin, the famous highwayman, rode his horse, Black Bess, up the stairs. I enjoyed several happy months there until I left to go to the Castle Hotel at Tamworth. This was a wonderful opportunity for me after living in Doncaster; I was going back home, back to the place where I had been so happy.

The Army Years

After finishing my time at the Castle Hotel in Tamworth I returned home with a heavy heart, with nothing to look forward to and no direction. I needed to find something to do with my time so I engaged in a window cleaning partnership with an old friend of mine and we cleaned the windows all around the village. Each afternoon I would go into the local betting shop and lose all the money that I had earned that morning by backing the horses. By Friday I had lost all of my money and when it came to the time for me to give my mother my housekeeping money for the week, I pretended that I had lost it somewhere. I would spend the next few hours wandering aimlessly around the village, looking for something that I knew it was impossible to find. I was seventeen years old and there seemed to be no point in my life. I owed the taxman for money from the betting office and I seemed to be permanently penniless.

One morning I had the inspirational idea that I would like to work with animals and decided that I would go along to the Army recruitment office and tell them that I wanted to be a dog handler. Yes, I could see myself with an Alsation and imagined how smart I would look walking the dog in my uniform, the folly of youth as they say. The Recruitment Officer soon put me straight. 'You can't just do that lad,' he bawled, ' you have to do basic training first and then join your Regiment.' Right then, I thought, I'll do that and then I will become a dog handler. Famous last words, as they say.

I joined the Regiment of 13/18 Royal Hussars, Queen Mary's Own. It was a tank regiment and off I went to Catterick Garrison in North Yorkshire to do my basic training as a tank gunner. All of a sudden my life was filled with excitement, running and cross-country, short hair cuts, lots of new friends and of course all of the discipline. I loved it. The best part for me was the boxing, I became the light welterweight champion of the intake but six months later I was posted to a place called Paderborn, in West Germany, to join my Regiment. I wore the Number One Dress, which consisted of a jacket with chain mail on the shoulders, white stripes down the trousers, white peaked cap, white gloves and spurs. It made me feel extremely smart and very proud. I spent the next three years doing a tour of active service in Berlin. Some of the time was spent patrolling the Berlin wall and guarding Spandau Prison, where Rudolph Hess had been incarcerated since the Second World War.

It was a short time later, during one of my home leaves, that I met my wife-to-be, Dorothy. We met at a local dance and she later wrote me a letter, asking me if I would like to get married and I said that I would. I flew home and caught a train from Manchester. During the journey I was watching a group of men playing cards, they were playing a game called 'Find the lady.' Ever the gambler, I joined in with these con men and consequently lost all my money for the wedding. I borrowed the money from a friend once I reached home but dare not tell my wife about this until many years later. It was then that I made the decision that I would buy myself out of the army, I rarely saw my new wife and there was no army accommodation available for us.

However, this plan did not work out either as we were all called to parade to be informed that trouble had broken out in Aden and that volunteers were needed. All volunteers were asked to take one step forward; it would not have been honourable for me to buy myself out at this time so I stepped forward. During the tour of Aden I was on escort duties and the enemy were mortar bombing a place called Regal Roundabout; I was escort on a Landrover and we stopped about half a mile away.

From this point in the desert scrubland I could see an Arab who was firing mortar bombs, I lifted my rifle and had him directly in my sights. I radioed back to Headquarters, 'Permission to fire,' I asked. 'Permission NOT GRANTED,' was the reply. As I have looked back over the years those words have echoed in my ears. I was not happy about it at the time, but I now thank God that I was not allowed to do it. It was not under my control as to whether to kill that man or not, indeed he may have killed me, but I do know now, that I would have had to face him at a later spiritual time. This incident earned me the nickname 'Bullets McGuire,' and it went into despatches and was sent to my wife at home. On returning to England I finally paid the money and I bought myself out but I never did get the opportunity to become a dog handler. I would like to add that there would be many readers who have served in the Forces, and will have been engaged in battle and taken a life. You must not attach guilt to this, as you did this not out of malice, but for the freedom and protection of others. You may have to meet that person at a later spiritual date, but the reasons that you did it are known.

I had numerous jobs upon leaving the army, every one of them low paid. The first was in a flourmill, which was very monotonous and then I worked for a tractor firm and finally moved to more decent employment, working for ICI. Our eldest son, Robert, was then born, shortly followed by our second son, Martin. We never seemed to have much money in those days, even though I worked long hours. We could only afford a tiny house and life seemed to be all about work. Our saving grace was that my wife was very much a family woman and a good manager; she adored our two boys and held everything together. There were always nappies drying around the fireplace and the usual feeding, bathing and melee of family life. I, still in my infancy, was bored and used to go out at night to the local dances. I used to sit there, still bored and wondering what on earth I was doing there. I seemed to be looking for something; something was certainly missing from my life.

It was not long after this point that I felt drawn to go to the Spiritualist Church, where these thoughts came from I do not know, just that a strong force was driving me to go there. It was unexplainable and sounds highly unlikely for a character such as me, but I went with the feeling. I now know that I was being taken on a journey of no return, in order to start the most important work of my life. I was destined to work for God. You may scoff at this, thinking how a character such as me, a biker, a gambler and a bit of a wrong'un all round could come to go inside a Spiritualist Church. It has taken me many years to learn that we know very little about ourselves or the Universe and when God calls it is our instinct to answer, even when we have no idea what we are doing. Never underestimate yourself my friends, for God loves all, no matter what others may think.

The Spiritualist Church

I had a desperate urge to go to the spiritualist church and why I did not know, I just knew that I had to follow my instincts and go there. I found myself day after day, looking at the notice boards outside the church, but dare not venture inside. When I eventually plucked up the courage to actually go in I found it quite an ordinary and peaceful place. There were a group of ladies, who were sat in a circle and seemed to be having a meeting. I must have looked an unlikely candidate stood at the door in my black biker trousers but I went over to one of the women who informed me that this was a private meeting but that I was most welcome to come back to church on the Saturday as that was an open evening. I couldn't wait for Saturday to arrive, I felt really excited and changed into more suitable attire this time; off I went to my very first circle.

For anyone who is unfamiliar with the Spiritualist Church, there are evenings when everyone sits in a large circle, with all the lights on, to work with Spirit. During a Sunday service everyone sits in rows as usual. As I looked around at all the people in there I noticed that they were a very mixed bunch, of all ages and nationalities. I must admit I felt a little strange and nervous at this point and asked myself several times what was I doing here. The service opened with a prayer, then everyone said The Lord's Prayer and we sang some hymns. I did notice that everyone was sitting with their hands on their knees, palms upwards, so I copied them and did the same. We were then asked to sit in quiet meditation.

I sat there during the meditation, not really knowing what was going to happen, I just closed my eyes the same as everyone else, but all that I could see was black, no colours or anything, just the normal blackness. A woman in the circle stood up and came over to me. She said that she could see nuns in black habits walking around me and said that I had known someone called Ethel from when I worked in the Nottingham area. I told her that I had worked there, but I didn't know anyone of that name. The message went on to say that I had healing in my hands. I could not believe any of this, I was a bit of a rogue in those days, my thoughts were about motorbikes not healing, but I thanked her and she sat down again. The meeting went on for another half an hour, at which point I suddenly felt my jaw going numb; it was if I had been to the dentist and had a local injection. I kept rubbing it but it would not go away. I enjoyed the rest of the meeting and had a cup of tea and a chat with everyone.

That night my mind was churning over so much that I couldn't sleep. How could I be a healer? Who was the lady called Ethel that was mentioned? The numbness in my jaw was still irritating me. The day after the meeting, I bumped into one of my colleagues from work and I mentioned to him about my jaw still feeling numb. 'It's okay Mick, you are a sensitive,' he told me. He explained that 'sensitives', pick up on the conditions of other people and told me that someone in the church will have been to the dentist that day. He told me that if it happened again, that I must, in my thoughts and prayers, accept the condition that I have received and ask for it to be taken away. He told me that I must also ask for healing for the person who has the condition. It was very difficult to take in what he was saying to me, but he was a good friend, so I thought that I would do as he said. I sat in my chair when I got home and said a little prayer. I accepted the condition and asked for it to please be taken away and the numbness disappeared immediately and my jaw returned to normal. I was absolutely astonished. My explanation to rationalise this was that I had somehow hypnotised myself but I was not so sure that my rationale was correct. It was a strange concept for me to absorb.

It had certainly planted a seed of curiosity in my mind. Back at work, we were discussing the meeting during lunch and I stated once again that I did not know anyone of the name Ethel. 'Yes, you do,' said my mate Bill, 'what about when you worked at Tamworth Castle? You said that the person who was watching over you was Queen Aethelfleda,' (pronounced Ethelfleda). A shudder went down my spine, this lady had never occurred to me. She had made herself known to me once again and a pattern seemed to be emerging in my life with this lady at the centre of it.

The Development Years

It was the church that opened all the doors for me, inviting me to attend the open circles and the development circles and I learnt so much from the good people there. It is so important to have the church as a foundation, as it is the foundation for good. I also visited other spiritualist churches in the area to see how other groups worked. At home I meditated as they had taught me, closing my eyes and looking into my third eye. This lies in the middle of the forehead and is the centre of spiritual development. It is the third eye chakra, and its colour is indigo. I still did not see anything through it, just black.

One day while sitting in the open circle at Bentley Spiritualist Church I remember feeling frustrated as all that I could still see was the black. I continued quietly meditating and resigned myself that this was all that I would ever see. I seemed to forget myself for a moment and suddenly a picture emerged. It was like looking at a television set. There was a snow scene with ice flows and an Eskimo paddling by in his kayak. One lady said that she had gone very cold, to which I piped up, 'Yes, that is your Eskimo guide.' 'Yes, I know,' she replied. She knew, she knew. I was jubilant; I had actually given a message. Wow. It was just as if someone had switched on a television set and all of a sudden getting a picture, it was truly amazing but I kept wondering if I had imagined it. Had I really given a message, it made me feel so elated and excited. In bed that night I relived the experience over and over again, how fantastic to be able to give a message.

During my sleep I found myself stood on the shore of the sea. On the beach were hundreds of people. They were telling me that they had come to watch me walk on the water. Me, walking on water, that is ludicrous, I thought and I then had the feeling that I could not let these people down; they were expecting me to do this. As I looked into the water, just under the surface there were lots of ships' masts. They were all joined together and stretched right out into the sea. I thought, I can fool these people, I can walk on the masts, and they will think that I am walking on water. I did this and they all applauded. A huge surge of guilt swept over me, I was utterly disgusted with myself, I had deliberately deceived all these people and I felt so ashamed.

At that point I heard my son Robert and he was drowning and was shouting hysterically for me to help him. I rushed in to the water and tried to get a hold of his hand and I then saw my youngest son, Martin and he too was drowning. I reached out to grab him with my other hand and as I did so I glanced down into the sea. The ships' masts were gone and I was actually walking on the water to save my son. It was a vivid dream and I woke up remembering every detail of it and I began to analyse all of the details. Perhaps the message that I had given at the church last night was not Spirit inspired, but just I kidding everybody. The latter part of the dream, when I really did walk on the water meant that I would give messages that were actually from Spirit and God. This explanation seemed right, I was always taught that if something felt right to accept it and if it felt wrong to reject it, so I accepted to myself that this is what the dream meant.

The following Sunday I went to the service as usual at College Road in Doncaster and found a seat at the back near to the door. The speaker was a woman called Margaret Pearson from Scarborough, a well-spoken lady who gave out really nice philosophy. Her first message was for me. 'Can I come to the gentleman at the back please, the one near to the light switch at the door.' I looked around. 'Yes, you sir in the leather coat,' she emphasised. It was me that she wanted. Her first words to me were, 'You have had a dream, haven't you.' I was stunned to say the least, as the dream was the first and foremost thing in my mind. She carried on with the message. 'I have your grandfather here, his name is William,' which shook me to the core. 'He is telling me about your dream. He tells me that you have interpreted it correctly. Well done,' she concluded.

I thanked her but sat there silently astonished; it was quite unbelievable, how could she possibly know about the dream? Spirit even knew what I was thinking at night and the seeds were once again sown. I knew then that I was being guided and had started upon a journey to investigate my own spirituality. The spiritualist church quickly became a huge part of my life and was all that I thought about. I attended all the development circles and the open circles, trying to learn everything that I possibly could. I went to every church within our area and was eventually allowed into the minister's circle. This was the top circle that encompassed people, who were potentially very good psychics. It was an honour and an experience that I could not wait for.

Harold Barnett, the minister, was a quiet unassuming man; he was one of life's great teachers. We all come upon people like him at some point in our lives and they make such a difference to our development. He would work with us for a little while, but then would allow us to work alone. It was his belief that it was not always the best thing to tell people what to do all the time; he said that it was better to let them learn to move along their own pathway, adding a little guidance here and there. He thought that it was very important to build a steady, firm foundation of learning which would stand you in good stead for future years. He said that the ones who tried to rush their teachings would soon flounder and that dedication and great patience were required.

This was a good early lesson for me as I was quite headstrong and wanted to learn everything immediately. I watched the healing group with an avid intensity. This field of work was my passion. I went to watch different individuals working and studied their different methods of working. Each healer had their own stool and people could sit wherever they chose, to have healing with whomever they felt the most comfortable. Of course all the healers were dedicated and caring people, who were very skilled at their work; it had taken them many years to accomplish their skills.

Eventually the time came when I was able to have my own stool. My particular stool always seemed to be full and this caused a certain amount of embarrassment for me, as people would wait in my queue when other stools were empty. It was not a very nice thing for them to do really, but it was also lovely to feel so wanted. It certainly encouraged me in my work, it is a wonderful thing in life, and to feel needed and wanted gives us all joy. This is the way that healing made me feel, that I had so much to give.

Harold Barnett was a trance healer, which means that he would allow Spirit to come through him to speak to the person concerned. It was amazing to observe.

He had two guides for the healing, an Egyptian doctor named Base Lara and the witty and charming Doctor MacGregor, a Scottish fellow with a very pronounced accent. The old ladies were mesmerised by the minister, they thought that he was marvellous. They would nod their heads and smile sweetly when Doctor MacGregor came through. 'Keep having a wee tipple dearie,' he would say and they loved him for it. It was my job at that time to heal the knees and ankles. I would be down upon my knees, laying hands on the old ladies' knees and ankles. They would scowl at me and brush me off, 'get off, get off,' while at the same time smiling sweetly at the wonderful Doctor MacGregor. I did not budge, my healing was powerful and they were getting it whether they liked it or not.

I have to smile at the memory of it now, the old ladies wanting the minister to do their healing, not a minion like me. My healing just grew stronger and stronger and the more that I used it, the stronger it became. The minister allowed me to take the rostrum now on a Sunday evening. I would do some trance work, giving a little philosophy and maybe two messages and then he would take over the service. I was very proud that he had taken such an interest in me and helped me so much, as he was very much a gentleman and always encouraged me to go forward. He told me that whatever happens in our lives, we must always go forward, never back.

I sometimes sit and ponder about how my development took place, and all the kind people who went out of their way to help me. They made me do the work that I needed to do to progress. Nothing in life that is worthwhile comes easily or without effort. The minister told me that I had worked slowly and steadily and had built a good foundation and that I would not be a two-minute wonder. Finally came the day when I took the rostrum alone, serving various churches, and as I sat there my thoughts turned to Jesus, the great teacher himself, and all the miracles that were possible through the channels of healing. It excited me beyond belief that Spirit and their healing power were now such a big part of my life and I waited in eager anticipation for all that was before me. I knew for certain that Spirit would walk the path with me, guiding and teaching me every step of the way.

A Dear Friend: Billy Dutton

This story is about a man who became a very dear friend of mine, Billy Dutton. Billy had recently lost his wife and was having a very bad time getting over his loss. One day as he took his daily walk he found himself outside the Spiritualist Church, just as I had done. He didn't know why, but day after day he felt drawn to the place. I was standing outside the door and he asked me if I would go in with him, as he didn't feel comfortable going in alone, this was the beginning of a wonderful friendship.

He said the church felt like he was going home, the sense of peace and belonging that he felt as soon as he entered. It was here at a later time that we both discovered that we were healers. Spirit teaches us that nothing in life is sheer coincidence and my meeting with Billy Dutton that day was most certainly arranged at a higher level.

At one of the meetings the speaker came over and told me that I had 'come here under the red light,' and that I should 'go back to the blue light.'

I didn't have a clue what she was talking about so she explained that the red light is for psychic work and the blue light is for healing. She told me that once I went back to the healing side then I would do the psychic work as well.

This was most surprising as I had been at home thinking cockily to myself that I would be one of the mediums on the stage but was told in no uncertain terms to get back to the healing, Billy found this very amusing.

Billy was a joiner by trade but was also informed by the church that he had healing abilities. We used to go to the church every week to observe the healers and then afterwards down to the pub to discuss what we had seen. Billy and I eventually had our own sanctuary at my home and we worked there for many years.

Billy's healing guide was Chinese and I watched with amazement as Billy tapped his hand on the patient while he was healing. I asked him why he did this and he said that the Chinese healers used to bang little bags of sand along the patient's body and his guide was using this technique through Billy.

Sadly my dear friend has now passed to the spirit world and he visited my writer, when she first started this book. She simply described to me that she had seen a man's face as she awoke, a man with a hole in his nose, she didn't take much notice of it the first time and then he came again.

I said 'Billy Dutton, well I never.' The description of him was unmistakable and Ann had never met him. I think that maybe he came so that we would not forget to mention him in the book. I could never forget you old friend. We shared a long and pleasant journey and after you passed, I sat thinking of you one evening and penned the poem 'Alone', which I dedicate to you.

God Bless you dear friend, till we meet again.

Harry Edwards
World-Renowned Healer

I never saw any real miracles happening in the Church but what I did see was people receiving comfort, either by the receiving of a message or the laying on of hands, their faces made easier by singing a hymn or saying a prayer. I was however extremely intrigued by the healing and could not get enough of the teachings. I attended church regularly every Saturday and Sunday evening and Thursdays for the teaching sessions. Everything that happened there fascinated me. Things also seemed to be happening to me at home, I was having strange dreams, as if somehow contact was being made and a spiritual door was opening. The possibility of being able to heal someone, to help someone was first and foremost in my mind, I could think of nothing else.

Time passed on and during one weekly service it was announced that Harry Edwards, the world-renowned healer was to do a demonstration at Sheffield City Hall. The church was going to send for some tickets and wanted names of anyone who would like a seat on the coach. I was like a boy at Christmas as I had heard so much about this great man and all of the miracles that he had performed; I was not going to miss this for anything.

I asked my mate Billy if he would come along with me but he wasn't too keen on the idea, he thought that he would not see anything different there to anywhere else. He said 'No, I am not bothered Mick, there won't be anything there to see, it will be just like in our church'. I told him that I felt sure that we would see miracles there but Billy still insisted that he was not going. I bought him a ticket anyway and thought that I would cajole him into going because I knew that he would be sorry later if he missed it. So off we went to the City Hall and what a revelation this night turned out to be.

I watched a middle aged man come onto the stage dressed in a white coat. He began by calling people up on to the stage to straighten arthritic joints and necks that could not move. Spinal misalignments were corrected and everything that he did, he did with such compassion and love. He gave out real hope. The crowd watched him in awed silence and I cried unashamedly all the way through. I knew this man worked with God, he performed miracle after miracle on the stage that night. I knew that this is what I had been searching for; this man, Harry Edwards; he was a true healer. He was the example that I had been looking for; he could do all these wonderful things to help people. It was the first time I suppose that I had seen anything with real substance in healing and what we would say is God's work. This was truly the work of a great man working for a loving God.

I went outside the City Hall and bumped into a young lady, who had a plaster cast on her leg. I joked with her and asked if she had come to get her broken leg mended. She replied that she had been in a wheelchair for ten years with multiple sclerosis and that Harry Edwards had cured her and she now went to all of his demonstrations. She toddled off down the road, quite unperturbed by the pot on her leg.

As she went off into the distance, I put my hands together and prayed; I felt that this was the time to start my healing crusade. I said to God that I would dedicate twenty years of my life to Him, to His healing and that all that I wanted was one cure, one miracle and if He would send the people to me, I would give them my love and my time to help them.

Harry Edwards died on December 7th, and on December 27th he visited me at night. He said that he had come to talk to me about the healing. His exact words were, 'When you are a healer, people will know it.' He put his hands on me and a force went through me stronger than anything I have ever known and he has worked with me ever since that day. I was told that I was the second Harry Edwards and I know that his spirit is with me all the time that I am healing, he is my teacher and guide.

I was taught the art of bone manipulation through Spirit and my guides have taught me lots about the human body and its conditions. I always work in a holistic manner, speaking to the person first about their background and what is happening in their lives. The mind, body and spirit all work together. When one is out of harmony so will the other be. I know that I am extremely privileged to have a great teacher such as Harry Edwards working with me. God bless him for all the wonderful work that he did here on Earth and continues to do in the spirit world. I send to him my prayers of love and the greatest respect.

Accept the Unexplainable

When I was about thirty years old, one of the very first circles that I sat in was where a brilliant trance medium worked. Her name was Beryl Stora and hers was an extremely inspiring circle, where many famous people came through. This circle was where I was introduced to Red Feather, the Indian guide of Beryl Stora, who was later to be my guide also.

A German doctor called Herr Schmidt also came through Beryl. He had been a surgeon during his lifetime and gave out a tremendous amount of power and talked about doing the healing through me. As the day ended and we went on our different ways, I decided to call in at the pub for a drink before I went home. It was a pub in Bentley called The Good Companions.

It was Bingo night and there was only one seat left available in the entire room. There were a few people sat around the table and I asked if they would mind if I joined them. I sat next to a woman about fifty years old who had a surgical collar around her neck and a badly deformed hand. She had a pen slotted between her fingers to play the bingo game. I did not say anything but I knew that this woman was in need of urgent help.

I sat listening to their conversation but could not really join in, as I had never met these people before. They mentioned the 13/18th Royal Hussars; that was my old Regiment and I heard her say that her son was in that Regiment too. I told them that this was my old Regiment and we talked for a while about the army and army life. Then right at the end of the evening, during a lull in the conversation, I asked the lady about her condition. She said that she had fallen down the stairs, when she was a fifteen-year-old girl and that gradually over the years everything had seized up. Her fingers were now shut tight and she could not open her hands; she also had a paralysed arm and a lot of pain in her neck. I could see that she had gangrene in one of her fingers and she told me that it was about to be amputated.

I told her that I was a healer and asked if she would like me to treat her and she said that would be lovely and asked where she could see me. I told her that I would see her at the end of the night outside and would give her some healing. Normally I would have asked her to come along to my sanctuary but this lady's need was great and I thought that I might not see her again. She accepted my offer of healing, although it must have seemed a little bit strange coming from a complete stranger sitting at the side of her. I met her and her husband outside and I asked her to put out her hand and I then closed both of my hands around her fingers. They were shut tight with all the muscles contracted, as she had not opened them for many years. I could feel the surge of electricity going through my hands into hers; I lifted my top hand off and her hand opened up to about fifty per cent. Her husband stood at the side looking on in absolute amazement and he asked me how I had done it. I went down her arm with my hands and then asked her to lift the arm up. She had never lifted them for as long as she could remember. Her home had been adapted to cope with her disability; all the kitchen cupboards were positioned at waist level for easy access for her. I asked her to lift the arm up and she went to lift it with her other arm but I told her, no, that she had just to lift the arm itself up. She looked at me with disbelief. The arm went straight above her head. Her husband started jumping up and down, "Can you do anything for her neck?" he asked me. I told him to remove her collar and, as I touched her, rigidity went and she was able to move the neck around. These were wonderful, amazing miracles, so awesome that I could not believe it myself; we all stood there in absolute amazement. I remember that I did not have my car that night, so the kind people offered me a lift home.

I did not sleep for the next three nights; I couldn't because of the excited thoughts going around in my head. I tossed and turned all night long; I had too many questions to ask to be able to sleep. Why could I do all these things? Did the German doctor, Herr Schmidt, work through me? Why was I always at the right place at the right time for someone to receive healing, who desperately needed it? I felt so unworthy to have this incredible gift but at the same time dizzy with excitement. I knew now that this was my life's mission, my spiritual quest.

The next time that I saw these people was once again in the pub. I was sat at a different table this time but noticed that they were looking over at me. The husband walked by me first of all and I caught a hold of his arm and told him that I knew that he was having difficulty accepting what had happened the week before but not to worry about it, just to accept it. He said that he could not believe that a stranger had come into the pub and sat next to them, taking his wife outside and performing a miracle with her. He told me that it had given her so much hope; she had started to massage her hands and move around so much better. He said that the only explanation that he had for the experience was that I had hypnotised them all. I shook my head and told him that I had not done that but it made me realise that, when miracles happen in front of people, how difficult it is for them to accept. How difficult it is to accept the power of God, for it was not any power that I have that cured this lady but the power of God.

It is very difficult for us to comprehend these things, as we are conditioned not to. If we cannot find a logical explanation for something, we are taught not to accept it; even if we can see the proof before our very eyes.

It does not matter though because the lady now has a better quality of life, thanks to the power of God. That is good enough reason for me to continue with my work, I do not need to justify what is happening, the results speak for themselves.

Death Where is Thy Sting?

Billy Dutton knew a lady who had been a medium for many years and was a long-standing friend of his family, so he booked me in one night to see her. She seemed very pleasant and sat me down in her sitting room for the reading and picked up straight away on my vibrations, telling me that I was a healer. She told me that my grandmother was around me all the time and that she used to scour her doorstep with a piece of sandstone. This was exactly right, I remember her doing it when I was a child. The rest of the message was very clear and she ended it by saying that I must listen very carefully to my grandma. I was a little bit too sure of myself in those days and I sort of said 'Yes, yes,' but did not really pay any heed to what she was saying. Mrs. Mea saw this and said it more emphatically this time, 'You must listen to what your grandma is saying to you, she is here to prove something to you,' she told me.

She went on. 'There is something else that I want you to remember.' Her words were quite forceful now, so I sat up straight. 'She would not hurt you when she was alive, and she will certainly not hurt you now that she has died. Remember those words, they are important.' I went home that night with the words of the old lady still going around in my head. I wondered what my gran was going to show me but I felt very happy that she was still around me, it was lovely to know that, and I had loved her dearly.

I was on afternoon shift the following day and woke up in the morning with a really dry mouth. I could hear my wife downstairs getting ready for work and I called to her to put the kettle on for me, as I wanted a cup of tea. I remember her shouting that she did not have the time as she was going to work and then the door closed and she was gone. The next thing that I knew I was in a small village, the village where my grandma was born, it was called Tollbar. I seemed to be gliding above the pavement, not touching anything. I passed by all the houses and the paper shop. The paper shop had been gone for a long time, but the billboards were outside.

What on earth was happening to me? I pinched myself, and it hurt, this was really happening to me, I was not dreaming. I passed by my grandfather's house, I call it this because my grandma had died many years before and I was used to my grandfather living there alone. I went to the door, but there were two doors and I couldn't understand this. I slipped my hand in the first door to try to open the second one and just managed to get my hand inside. The place was really noisy and yet this was odd as the house had always been a calm, quiet place.

As I looked up I got the shock of my life. There at the top of the stairs was my grandma, I recognised her instantly, although she looked very different. She had died from cancer and had been ravaged by the illness but now she looked radiant and beautiful and about twenty-three years old. Her red hair was fastened up in clip curls, as they used to do in her days. She had on a sort of corset type top and in her left hand was a candleholder with a brightly burning candle in it. She started to walk down the stairs, I was terrified and turned to run away but Mrs. Mea's words suddenly came into my head, 'She would not hurt you when she was alive and she will not hurt you now that she is dead.' Her words gave me courage and I stood there, quite still. I expected her to come towards me, but she turned around and went into the lounge. She placed the candleholder upon the table, which had a dark green, velvety tablecloth on it with tassels hanging down. She then went to stand by the fire; it was the old black oven and range. She warmed herself and looked straight at me, and I at her, but she did not give me any response. I tried to say something but nothing came out of my mouth, then the words seemed to come from the left hand side of me. 'I'm here Gran, aren't you going to give me a hug?' She picked up on it and started to walk towards me. I was trembling now and wished that I had not said anything but I thought that she could not touch me because she was a ghost. She took hold of my hand and cupped it in her two hands, she felt warm, solid and wonderful. I felt the tears start to flow; I had loved her dearly during her life and was devastated when it ended.

The next minute I was back in my bed, I woke up with my hands on my head. Every minute of the time that I had spent with her came back to me. I saw everything in fine detail, her clothes and shoes. I saw the pots and pans and the tiles on the floor. I could see her washing machine and all her ornaments and pictures. I could see her iron statues in the hallway upstairs and her lovely garden. I was so excited and ran downstairs missing half of the steps. I now had proof beyond doubt that life exists beyond this one, I had held my grandma's hand and it was the greatest revelation of all time to me.

I told Dorothy that evening, while she was drying the dishes from the supper, 'I saw my gran, I really saw her, and I even felt her, solid and warm.' 'Oh yeah?' she replied unconvinced. It did not matter; I knew what I had seen.

At work the next day, I told all of my colleagues. They shook their heads and I could see what they were thinking, 'Mick has gone barmy.' Nobody wanted to listen to me; they all thought that I was mad. It really hurt, because I wanted so much to share this experience with everyone, to assure them that I knew that we did not die.

Eventually I had to take it as a personal experience, it is hard when people don't understand and no one was prepared to even listen to me. I had crossed over a barrier; I saw my gran who was not ill but young and full-bodied, I just wished that the world could only see what I saw. This would never be enough now, I knew that, I wanted to know more, much more. Thank you Gran for that wonderful moment in my life, for proving to me without a shadow of a doubt, that life goes on; our spirit lives on. I know this and no one can ever take it away from me now, because I was there. Death where is thy sting?

Serving in the Churches

I was now serving in most of the churches within the Yorkshire area and went this particular evening to the Spiritualist church in York, which is a beautiful church, exuding a wonderful feeling of peace. I stood upon the rostrum and offered a small prayer and gave a little philosophy before commencing with the psychic work.

A gentleman, dressed in a suit appeared at the door and was carrying a duck. He walked down the aisle and stood at the side of a woman in the audience and waited patiently for me to tell her that he was here and to acknowledge his presence. I held out my hand and asked if I could please come to the lady sat at the end of the aisle. 'A gentleman has just walked in and stood beside you, and under his arm he is carrying a duck.' The audience all started to laugh. The woman did not laugh though; she looked very serious and asked me if it was a duck or a goose. I looked further and told her that yes, she was right, it was indeed a goose, it was the Christmas goose that he had under his arm. 'I believe that this man is your husband.'

The audience were still laughing, which was quite rude of them. They thought that this was some sort of joke. The lady stood up from her seat and asked everyone to please be quiet. 'You are all laughing, but this is quite correct,' she said. 'My husband and I used to keep geese. One of the geese used to follow me around, it became like a family pet.'

'One Christmas morning I was in the kitchen preparing Christmas lunch, I was peeling the potatoes and cutting the sprouts, when my husband walked in and under his arm was my pet goose, he had killed it for our dinner. The day that this happened I became a vegetarian and have been one ever since. So you see, it may seem a funny message, but I know that it is my husband stood here beside me.' Maybe he had come back to say sorry for killing the goose, or maybe it was to say that they were now together in the spirit world. The woman was very grateful for the simple message that I brought and said that it meant a great deal to her.

It was during another service one Sunday evening that my first link with Spirit was for an elderly lady who looked around eighty years old. As I began to give off the message an overwhelming feeling of sadness swept over me. I could see a glass of water and some tablets on the bedside cabinet. I turned to the lady and asked quietly, 'Tell me dear, are you going to do something when you go home tonight?' She put down her head and replied, 'Yes, I am.' I felt that it would be unethical to give off this message in front of the audience so I asked if I might speak to her at the end of the service. I told her that it was very, very important that I did so.

I knew that this lady intended to take her own life that night and had put everything ready by the bedside. I could not let that happen, but I felt that it was not for public knowledge. This service could not end quickly enough for me. I was so eager to speak to her; I kept a constant eye during the other messages to make sure that she did not leave the church. I eventually managed to take her into a quiet corner and made sure that my manner was gentle. 'You are going to kill yourself tonight aren't you, my friend?' 'Yes, I have got everything prepared,' her voice was barely a whisper and I asked her to please tell me why. This was the story that she went on to tell me.

A few weeks previous, she had gone into a shopping centre in Rotherham and walked into an electrical store. While she was in there, she stole a large standard lamp, this little old lady was only five feet high and she had walked into the shop and picked up the huge lamp and walked out with it. The store detective who then arrested her caught her outside and she was later charged with shoplifting.

I asked her what had made her do it but she didn't know, she could not even remember doing it. She went on to tell me that her husband was in his nineties and was bedridden, he was terminally ill and she was caring for him on her own.

It was actually a cry for help, but there was no one to listen. She had found herself outside the store with the lamp in her hand; it was a momentary lapse of mind due to all of the stress that she was under. The shame of it all had suddenly hit her and the poor lady, thinking that she may go to jail had decided to take her own life. I asked her which solicitors were working for her, but she did not have any. She was due to be in the courts the following week and wanted to kill herself before it came to that stage.

I told her that killing herself was definitely not the answer. There were people out there who would understand her predicament and would most certainly help her. They would realise that she had not done it deliberately and that it was all a dreadful mistake. I asked her would she please go to the Citizens Advice Bureau, and tell them the story that she had told me and assured her that they would be able to help. I talked to her for quite a long time and she seemed to be in a happier frame of mind. I was satisfied that I had reassured her enough that she would not do anything silly and she promised me that she would take some advice.

Two weeks later, I received a beautiful letter from her. She did what I asked and had visited the Citizens Advice Bureau in Rotherham. She said that they were really helpful and arranged for her to see a solicitor. The solicitor assured her that she did not need to attend the courts and that he would sort it all out on her behalf. They also arranged for Social Services to visit and arrange for some help with the care of her husband.

Life had overwhelmed her and it was too much for a lady of her years to cope with. Once again Spirit had intervened to help with a suicide and I pray to God that no matter what age we are, that we do not commit suicide. Instead of doing this we need to search and keep on searching for the help that we need. Someone, somewhere will have the answer.

I personally have given a great deal of thought to the subject of euthanasia. We read stories in the paper of people who are terminally ill, who have gone off to foreign places to have their lives terminated. I have recently read that some of the people who did this turned out not to be terminally ill after all. I do not want to see people die by their own hands by committing suicide.

We need to search for cures for people who have serious illnesses, to give healing and to pray for them, to try to alleviate their suffering as much as possible. I know that we terminate the lives of animals and we do not let them suffer but should we take it upon ourselves to do the same to human beings? It is a very complex area and we all have our own opinions about this, but my belief is that is it not for us to make that decision. I know from what I have been taught by the spirit world that our time here on Earth is fixed and we need to be here for the completion of our journey. I feel very strongly about someone else taking a person's life, as we will see more of this happening, in more and more parts of the world. What guidelines will be drawn and what errors will there be. When we go and it is not our time, we can be lost between the two worlds. I only pray that Spirit can help these souls to move on.

We live in a very strange world and some of the questions are very hard. We may feel that because of our problems we want to opt out, thinking that this is the easy option. Even on the computer network there are clubs of people, who want to find out how to kill themselves. I read a report recently, where two young men had decided to jump off a cliff. The last thing that they did was to telephone their friends to say goodbye. One good friend had talked one of them out of doing it and the other would not listen and jumped off a cliff. The other then killed himself a few days later. This then requires more work from the psychics and mediums, as these people can be trapped between the two worlds and must be rescued. They need help to move on into the light, into the spirit world.

The question of euthanasia is a very serious one and one that affects each and every one of us and the people that are to come after us. I feel that it will get worse and I sincerely hope that something can be sorted out before it does. I do not want it to get to the point of mass suicides, because there are lots and lots of people who are suffering, who are terminally ill. I am sure that there is a price to pay for man taking destiny into his own hands. For deciding the length of time that he spends upon the Earth plane. God Bless all the souls that have gone this way, I pray for the help of Spirit in the rescue of these people and that they may move on into the light.

"No Miracles at Work"

Life is a very unpredictable business and quite suddenly out of the blue our lives take on a different turn. We are settled and happy in the routine of our daily lives and very quickly everything changes. We find ourselves in a state of shock and sit down, deep in thought, trying to work out why these things have happened. Some situations have no logical explanation; it may be the loss of someone dear to us, an illness or a financial dilemma. All that we can do is to go forward and deal with the problem to the best of our ability. Our lives are all about learning. Though the healing Spirit has changed the lives of people instantly, they search for a logical explanation and the reasoning behind why they are suddenly better. They are sometimes afraid to tell others in case they are laughed at or disbelieved but all that they need to do is accept the fact that they are well again and give thanks.

This story is from when I was working at the ICI plant, I worked in the electrical section. The lads who worked there were a decent bunch and used to play cards during the lunchtime break, for money of course. Me, gambling again, I have always had a weak spot for a bit of a flutter. They were talking about a new bloke who was about to join the department. They had been told that he was a psychic and a healer. 'I'll bet we're all right with him,' one of the lads quipped, 'he'll be a right weirdo.' I carried on dealing the hand and told them that the man was me. I am the psychic and the healer. 'You Mick,' they said. 'Gerraway, it's not you.' They seemed quite alarmed and shocked that I was just an ordinary person but just shook their heads and carried on playing cards.

After the break I went back to my desk. As I sat there working on one of the lamps, one of the lads came over to me. He was a young man called Chris, a good-looking kid, really muscular; he always wore a vest to show off his physique. He said to me 'Mick, I have heard that you are a healer.' 'Yes Chris, I am,' I told him. He asked me if I could help him so I asked what the problem was. He said that he had got a deformed hand, he had broken his wrist and his hand would not straighten anymore and being an electrician he was in constant pain while he was working. He also told me that his girlfriend was visibly embarrassed by it. She asked him to use the other hand when they were out in company, or if he went to take change at the shops.

The young are very sensitive about these things. I told him that, if he came to me after work, I would see what I could do for him. He turned around and started to walk away, when the strangest thing happened. It seemed like I was sat behind a doctor's desk and I felt compelled to shout him back, which I did. Chris turned around and I asked him if I might look at his wrist. He held out his hand to me, and the instant that I touched his wrist he passed out. I jumped up from my chair to catch him and lifted him on to a stool. He was unconscious and his skin was very pale, sweat was pouring from his brow and dripping on to the floor. I called his name but there was no response. I took hold of his wrist to manipulate it but it was already straight, it was perfectly straight.

A group had gathered around us; the men wanted to see what was going on. They all looked really shocked and concerned for him. I didn't though, I felt relaxed and calm and Chris started to move and came round again. I asked him to look at his wrist and when he saw it he started to swear. He couldn't believe it and tried to run out of the room but I told him to sit still and stay with me; that in a few moments he would feel absolutely wonderful.

Just as this was happening, the foreman came through the door and saw the group gathered around me and Chris sat on the chair. 'What's going on here?' he bawled. I told him that it was okay, that Chris would be fine in a minute. He slammed the door behind him and went out again. A few minutes later Chris stood up and let out the loudest yelp, he threw his arms in the air and shouted that he had been cured. He went running all around the factory, into all the departments and the stores, waving his hand around and shouting it from the rooftops that I had cured him. About twenty minutes later, the head boss came in; he looked across at me and asked me to go into his office. I thought right, I am in trouble now. He ran his department with clockwork precision and wouldn't stand for 'troublemakers'.

I went into his office and closed the door and sat down. His first words to me were 'I am a non-believer.' I asked him what that was to do with me. He said, 'I don't know how you have done what you have just done but I cannot allow you to go around the factory making people unconscious.' I told him that I couldn't do that even if I wanted to. His name was Charlie and he was a nice guy.

He said to me, 'Look Mick, what you do in your spare time is up to you but do not do it at work,' and that was it and off I went. His words made me smile, 'No miracles on work premises, do them at home.' From that day on the men at work approached me with all sorts of problems, illnesses, relationships, and work problems. I don't know why I felt like a doctor behind the desk that day or why I had the sudden urge to call Chris back to me. It was mind-boggling to take in all these wonderful happenings. What I do know is that Spirit is capable of anything and that I am simply a channel for all of the work that is to be done. Since those first miracle things have happened like that time after time, I don't question them anymore; I just do the work as and when Spirit needs me.

'Operation Ocean'

There was an excellent camaraderie among the men at the ICI plant. We shared the ups and downs of our lives during the tea breaks, laughing and joking and sometimes covering serious issues. We all discussed our various hobbies and interests and most of the men knew of my involvement with the church and my psychic work and the healing and it was at this time that a friend of mine, Peter, became seriously ill and developed cancer. I kept on thinking to myself that I should go to visit him, but seemed to carry on with my daily routines, as people often do and never got around to it. Another mutual friend of ours called at my home after he had finished his shift at work and came to tell me that Peter's condition was now very serious. He said that the doctor did not hold out much hope that he would survive and could I go to see him as soon as possible. I promised him that I would, but three to four months passed by and I still had not been.

Our friend told me once again at work, that Peter now had only a short time to live and I said that I would definitely go to see him that night. I asked him, 'What would you say if Peter was alive in six months,' and he said that it would be a miracle. I remember sitting at home that night, and asking Spirit if they could cure cancer. I prayed and prayed. I silently asked Spirit 'Would you prove to me that we can do this, could you cure this cancer I will never doubt you ever again.'

Peter's wife answered the door upon my arrival; she showed me to his room upstairs and I was taken aback by his appearance. He looked nothing like the man that I had known.

Peter weighed about six stones and all his skin was tinged with yellow. His gaunt face stared at me with eyes that were full of fear. I put my hand upon his shoulder and told him that I had come to give him some healing. Peter and I talked for a while first and he told me that the jaundice was making his skin itch and he was scratching himself sore. I asked him to lie back and try to relax and to think of the colour blue. When my hand went to his head his face took on a more peaceful expression; his brow was not so tense and his jaw and mouth relaxed.

A kind of stillness, a peace, came about him until finally he stopped moving altogether and fell into a deep sleep. I could feel that the healing energies that were around him were very good and that Spirit was around. I asked Spirit that I may be used for a channel for his healing and healed him for about twenty minutes and then I stopped. He had gone into a deep sleep with no movement at all; he was totally still. I said a prayer to thank God for the minutes peace that he was having and asked Spirit to stay with him. The night nurse was due to come in a short time to watch over him, as the doctor had only given him a few hours to live. I went downstairs into the living room, where his wife made me a cup of tea, I told her that Peter was asleep now and that I would come again the following Friday to give him some more healing. I remember thinking that he would probably not be here. I went to work as usual but heard nothing of Peter's progress and assumed the worst.

Not knowing what awaited me, I went back the next Friday and his wife came to the door and told me that his condition was worse. He was now delirious and tearing up the blankets. His mind had gone and the doctor had told her that his time to pass was very close. I went into his room and looked at Peter; his eyes were wild and unseeing. As I moved forward I prayed that Spirit would be with me and would come forward to administer the healing.

Once again Peter fell into a deep, restful sleep and I could see all the beautiful colours surrounding him; all the wonderful healing that he was being given. The peace surrounding him was almost tangible, so I prayed again and asked for a miracle. The healing lasted for about twenty minutes; no twitching or scratching, just sleep and peace. I thanked God once again for the healing that He had sent. I went downstairs and chatted to his wife. She told me that the week before that Peter had slept for three and a half hours following the healing. She said that she knew that there was a strong probability that he would not be around the following Friday but I assured her that I would come anyway and prayed once more for a miracle to take place; that the Spirit doctors would help him. During the week again I received no news and the following Friday with a heavy heart I went to his house. I feared the worst and I took a few deep breaths before I knocked on the door.

Peter himself opened it, "Hello, Mick, come on in," he said and my jaw was on the floor, I was rendered speechless. Peter sat back at the kitchen table, where he had been eating a huge salad and we sat and had a bottle of Guinness together. In those days I smoked so we had a cigarette as well, just like the old days. He chatted ten-to-the-dozen and then told me the story of what had happened during the healing. Peter said that he remembered me putting my hands on him and the next minute he was on the ocean, on a boat. All the people on the boat were wearing white coats and he presumed that they were doctors. Also on the boat was his mother, who had been dead for a long time. She comforted Peter and helped while the doctors were working on him.

Peter looked so well now that I gave him healing from the chair. While I was giving the healing I could hear strange sounds coming from his bowels and stomach and his breathing altered. He had had surgery six months previous and was told that the cancer cells had invaded all of his organs. The strange noises carried on, but he seemed unperturbed by them. He seemed different, as if he had developed an inner strength. He was mentally much stronger and I knew somehow that Spirit had touched his soul.

He continued with the healing for many weeks and got

stronger and stronger, until finally he returned to total fitness. The odd thing was that no one questioned it. After being terminally ill, one would have thought that the doctors at the hospital would want to investigate the matter. When I asked for the miracle for Peter, his wife had been very poorly also with rheumatoid arthritis and I asked God to give Peter five more years.

My thoughts were all over the place. 'How wonderful God is, that he can cure this person,' and my faith was now indestructible. I knew from that moment that anything is possible, when working with God and I adhered to my promise to Him, that if I had a miracle, then I would serve Him for the rest of my life and this is what I have done. God's power is boundless, His love and His healing can cure any condition. I am awe-struck by God's miracles. They brought my grandmother from her deathbed, and now they had cured cancer, how great He is.

The Laying of Hands

This is the story of Hilda whose brother-in-law was a close friend of mine at the ICI plant. It was during one of our lunchtime conversations that he told me that Hilda had developed a very rare form of cancer; she had clusters of tumours in her stomach and was now terminally ill. He asked me what I would say to her if he brought her to see me and I told him that I would try to be honest and that is all. One Monday evening his car pulled up outside my drive and I saw him help Hilda out of it and escort her up the path to the house. When they came Hilda looked surprised, as I was playing a piece of classical music that she said was her father's favourite. I sat her down and asked her to tell me all about her illness. She had a scan taken at the hospital six weeks previous, which clearly showed all the evidence of the tumours.

I asked her to lie down on the couch and made her comfortable and began the healing. A Chinese gentleman came through, who said that his name was Ming and he was there to help to fight the cancer. I told Hilda this and she said 'How extraordinary, I have been sorting out the attic today, and I came across a Ming vase (a copy I presume), that I had forgotten was there. I held it in my hand for quite a long time.' The healing went very well but it was far too early to make any promises. She told me that she was due to go back to the hospital for further tests and the doctors were going to put an optic down her throat to photograph the growths.

In-between her hospital visits she came back for more healing and after about four weeks I felt that Spirit had cured her. I did not say anything; it was too early to be optimistic. Six weeks passed by and six healing treatments and Hilda was to go back to hospital that Friday, she was going for the results of the optic camera. She rang me that evening and said that she thought that she heard them say that they could not see anything. I told her just to wait and see because if they could not find anything, they would most certainly be back in touch with her. She received a letter a few days later, stating that she needed to go back to the hospital for further tests. They gave her an appointment for the following Tuesday. When these were completed she must return on the Friday for the results, it was a very harrowing time for her.

Friday came and it brought with it a beaming lady to my home. Hilda had seen the oncologist at the hospital and had been given the 'all clear', amazingly they could find no evidence of the tumours. She was bombarded with questions by the staff. Had she taken anything different, had she been for any sort of treatment? Hilda never mentioned the healing, she simply said 'No.'

The specialist asked if she would mind being examined by a Medical Board, as he found it inexplicable that the cancer had disappeared and obviously needed further opinions. The Medical Board looked laboriously through all of her notes and passed the photographs of the scan around. She was again examined and questioned and the doctors admitted that they were perplexed at the diagnosis but the healing was still never mentioned. Hilda was discharged but required to go to the hospital for regular checks to ensure that the tumours had not returned. Twenty-three years have passed and thankfully she remains well and still attends the Oncology Clinic once a year. They look at the notes and simply shake their heads in disbelief. People are very reluctant to believe that the laying on of hands can cure, even though it has been done since the time of Jesus and they feel afraid to speak to medical staff about it. I can fully understand this; it was not too long ago that I too knew nothing about healing. Now I want to shout it from the rooftops, it is for everyone, it is God's gift to all.

Committing to the Healing

After several years the healing began to be part of my life's structure, it was my pathway to God's work. I decided that it was the right time to leave my job at ICI and at that time redundancies were being given so I thought that if I could raise two or three thousand pounds, then this would be a very good start for me. Lots of my work colleagues were leaving, but every time I asked for redundancy I was refused. I could not understand why they would not let me go, when men were finishing every week, but every time they told me the same thing. I was looking around for another house, as I wanted a house that I could work from, just a small place, but with enough room to build a Sanctuary. I felt that it was time to do the healing full time. I had a lot of difficulties as my own house would not sell at first and it took a long time to find another home. At work they flatly refused to allow me to take redundancy, so I had to make the decision either to stay or just to leave of my own accord, to leave without any money or gratuity and no other job to fall back on.

I put all of my faith in Spirit, who said that everything would work out. I had already decided that this was the right time, it was time to take the giant leap of faith that was necessary to change my life, I knew without a doubt that Spirit would help and guide me all of the way, so I handed in my notice and finished work. We eventually sold our first home and moved into the new one. At last we were able to pay the people the money that we owed. I had to take out quite a large mortgage to get this house. I felt that I had completed my apprenticeship and now was the time to work on my own with Spirit, for God. I remember growing a beard and moustache, so that I would look older and more distinguished. It sounds silly now but I wanted to look the part so that people would have faith in me. I had different people working alongside me, starting with my friend Billy from the church and then Linda and Michael and Pat.

One evening a lady had booked in to see me, her name

was Mavis. She was a tall, elegant woman with a thick mane of black, wavy hair. I asked her into the Sanctuary for treatment and the moment she walked through the door she commented that she felt as if she had come home. She came back on quite a few occasions and gradually got better. She asked if she could come to help me with the healing and I told her that she could come for a trial on Saturday night and I would see how she got on, I wanted to observe if she could blend with the healing and work with it.

There were two ladies booked in for treatment, the first lady was in her thirties and was lying on the couch waiting for us. I placed my hands upon her neck and said to her that her father had passed away. I told her that he was here and that he loved her and that he was telling her not to weep because he was very happy. He said that she had financial problems, but in three months, they will all be sorted out. She looked quite amazed. I then went on to heal the next lady, who was a little older and as I lay my hands upon her Spirit came through once again. 'I have your child here with me. He passed away when he was six months old, and his name is John. He has grown in the Spirit world and has brought you the most beautiful bouquet of spiritual flowers.' It was huge; it must have been a yard in width. The colours in it were really vivid, blues, greens, reds and purples and an array of the most exotic flowers. She started to cry and nodded to me in acknowledgement.

When the healing was over Mavis went over to the two ladies to ask them if all this information was correct and they both confirmed everything that I had said. The seed was sown and Mavis was hooked, she said that she knew that she had found her vocation in life. She has been with me now for over twenty years, Spirit sent her to me, as she too was to spend the rest of her life working for God, helping and assisting me.

Mavis also has another role in my life. She has a very strong personality and is my protector; she wards off the people who try to abuse my kindness. I am not really a businessman, but a healer and there have been people who have tried to take advantage of this over the years. Mavis is a straight-talking, forthright lady and I have been thankful for that on many occasions. She directs people as a mother would her child, firmly but with no-nonsense. Sometimes I have been extremely tired and people have taken up too much of my time but Mavis always comes to the rescue, nicely but with no quarter given.

I believe that Spirit had chosen her personality for this role, as it would make for a proper balance in the work that we had to do. She is now in her seventies but is still absolutely devoted to our work and I know that she will never let me down. She works for Spirit and for God, not for me and protects me for the work that still has to be done. I know that she will be here alongside me, until her time or mine comes for us to pass over. She is my Spirit protector on the material plane and I owe her a great deal. She is the mother of the Sanctuary. I know that not everyone finds it easy to accept her frankness; sometimes the words just tumble out and Mavis has told someone what she thought, but there is never any malice, just honesty.

We did not earn very much money for several years in the new clinic. At the end of the day, I would pay the staff their wages and there was nothing left for me, but I found ways around this, I borrowed from the bank and I used my credit cards. The people kept on coming and I managed to pay the bills and survive for another year. My charges were still very small but as each year passed I learned a little more. There were examples of healing miracles happening all the time in the Sanctuary and each day I thanked God for His help. I was always very tired but I tried to serve as much as I was able. People seemed to need me, and while they needed me, I could not go home. I could not turn anyone away.

There were also many psychic incidents and sometimes I would sit alone and ponder, 'Is all this really happening to me or does it just exist in my mind. Is it real? Am I really being guided or am I just kidding myself?' I was always asking myself questions. Was I really a channel for all these miracles; me, an ordinary guy, but I just had to accept everything, as I could certainly not explain it.

I hope that in the next few chapters I can give you some idea of what it is like to work for God; to put your complete faith in God. It is very easy to have faith when everything is going okay and nothing is wrong. It is during the difficult times that our faith is put to the test; during the hard times in life such as bereavement and illness, that is when you need to know that you are never on your own. We all need to know that we can talk to God at any time of day or night. Wherever you are, in bed, even on the toilet, He is always listening. God will always help you and all that he asks is that you meet him half way, a fifty-fifty partnership. Self-responsibility and the guidance of God, how powerful a combination is that?

My life totally changed when the calling from God came and believe me I was quite a laughing stock. People told me that I was mental but I didn't care in the least. God had called me to do his work and I was not going to let Him down. Time moves on and Mankind has learnt so much and yet has so much to learn, we have not even begun to scratch the surface of the knowledge that is available to us, or of what is to come for us. If we all only realised that we have eternal life, a life that goes on for infinity, beyond the physical body. We are constantly learning about the world around us, about our emotions, and ourselves. There is so much to understand and to come to terms with; so many hurts to withstand and to overcome. The Earth is where our spirit comes to learn, it is our school and the place where our soul can evolve.

The one thing that stands out from all that we learn is that

LOVE is the greatest power of all. Love will see us through anything. Love is the power of God. I hope that by the end of this book you will have realised that you are never alone; God is always with you. Never underestimate the power of prayer my friend, for prayers are your conversations with God and I can assure you that He hears every word. Sometimes the answer may not be what you expected, but He knows the bigger picture and will always guide you in the right direction.

I hope that some of the chapters and stories in this book will inspire you and will move you on to a greater life with greater purpose. Maybe it will make some people realise that they are healers, even great healers. What legacy will you leave upon this Earth when you pass over to the spirit world. If you have helped just one person along their way then your visit here will have been worthwhile.

I know that everyone can heal and there are many ways to do this. To talk kindly to someone is giving healing words, comforting a child within the warmth of your arms is healing, stroking an animal, some people are wonderful animal healers. We all unconsciously heal every day. Give out your love and healing to all around you, to the plants, to the animals, to the fish, to the insects, to every living thing, especially each other. Send a thought out each day and say a prayer for healing to go all around the world, to wherever it is needed the most and know that your prayer will be heard. Go forward with positive and loving thoughts, in everything that you say and do, God will work with you and bless you all my dear friends.

Building the Sanctuary

The time was now right for me to start up my own healing sanctuary; my place to help all the sick and suffering and all that I needed was for God to send them, and I knew that He would do that. I enlisted the help of Billy and we set about converting the garage that was attached to my home. First of all we filled in the pit that was used to get under the car, and then we decorated the walls and added a new carpet. We picked fancy matching curtains for the window and the final touch was a cross upon the wall. All that I needed now was a couch but goodness knows where I would get that from, I certainly couldn't afford to buy one but my instincts told me that it would come and this is the story of how it happened.

As I was driving down the road one afternoon I glanced over at the gate to the local working-men's club and dumped outside the door, amidst all the rubbish was a wrecked old treatment table. I had a look at it but it was in a really bad state, so I went inside to ask to whom it belonged and was told that it had been used for years by the football team but was thrown outside to go to the rubbish tip. I asked if I may take it and then loaded it into the boot of my car. Billy was a joiner so I telephoned him to see if he could restore it for me. He worked wonders and after a few weeks work it was just like new and we now had our massage table.

Once anyone begins to work with God and Spirit, it focuses the mind towards a positive goal and then amazingly everything that is necessary takes place. I have used this table now for all the years that I have been healing and it is still in use in my Sanctuary in Doncaster.

We called our converted garage, The Healing Sanctuary. In the beginning we only healed in there for one night a week, then gradually as the word got around more and more people started to come to us. One of our neighbours stopped my wife in the street one day to ask what was I doing in the garage at night. They had noticed people going in and out. She told him that she didn't really know but said that it was a set of drums that I wanted last month, so goodness knows what the latest fad was. The cheeky monkey, I couldn't blame her, I was forever looking for my pathway in those days. Then the time came when we started travelling out to see people to heal them in their homes but there was never any charge, as I considered this my apprenticeship.

I have been very privileged and was taught so well in the church by Harold Barnett and the other healers, which gave me an excellent foundation of knowledge for my work. I also have the privilege of working with the great Harry Edwards, who teaches me from the higher side of life and all the other spiritual healers who have taught me so much. I know that I am truly blessed.

The Spiritualist Church is where everything in my life opened up for me. It is where I found my God, the God that I have now. I have been searching for this loving God for so many years. It is where I met my Spirit friends, who have been with me ever since. It is where I learned to work with my powerful guides and teachers, 'The Faceless One' and my powerful Indian guide and protector, Red Feather.

The most wonderful thing of all for me is the knowing that we do not die, but there is a life beyond, and most of all that there truly is a God. It is the most incredible feeling, a feeling of being eternally cared for and loved and also to know that our life here has a purpose; that we are here to learn all of the lessons that the Earth plane throws at us, in order to progress our souls. The most consistent message that I have been taught throughout all of my years working with the higher realms is to love, to love all, to love every living thing. I have had so many experiences in the field of healing, some of them small and some too huge for the mind to contemplate. I was shown the way by Spirit, for which I will be eternally grateful and I will of course dedicate all of my life to this end. I will continue to heal until the day that I pass over into spirit, hopefully teaching others on my path how we all have the ability to work with God. It is God's gift to us all; the ability to heal each other.

Forever
By Your Side

In my early years, when I was healing from the garage, a young couple came along for healing; they did not come for themselves, but for their bulldog. The dog was a show dog and they took him to competitions all over the country and his problem was that he had a limp. They always brought him for healing before a show and the healing would last for several days, the animal was never cured, just made better for a little while. He was a smashing little dog, really friendly and the couple had won several shows with him. Bob, the dog's owner, also came to me one day with a back problem; his lower back was very painful and it reached the point where he was coming to see me every day, each time that I answered the phone, it was Bob, asking to be seen again. I tried to tell him that he really ought to leave it for two or three days in between, to allow the nerves to settle down but he said that he could not manage. He crawled along slowly between the two houses to get to my garage; the poor chap was really suffering. It took a long time and a lot of patience, but we eventually got his back well again.

The story that I really want to tell you is about his wife Lyn. A number of years later, when I was working in the new clinic that I had bought, I received a telephone call from her asking for an appointment. This particular evening, the chiropodist, who also worked in our building had a problem with his car, the headlights were not working, so he could not drive home. The weather was dreadful that night and he decided that he would stay at the clinic until the morning.

When Lyn arrived, I did the physiotherapy first and then made her comfortable for the healing. It was only a few seconds into the healing that I noticed a really strong smell in the room, it was making me feel hungry, I also realised that there was the presence of a lady with Lyn. The lady had a bag of fish and chips in her hand and this was the mouth-watering aroma that I could smell. She kept wafting them temptingly under my nose and I remember thinking that she had put a lot of vinegar on them. I could have eaten them myself, as they smelled absolutely delicious. I explained to Lyn what was happening and told her about the fish and chips. 'I don't understand it Mick, I've no idea who it could be.' I wondered if the chiropodist who was staying for the night was hungry and had been to get himself a fish and chip supper, but he was sat there watching the evening news on the television. For any readers who do not live in England, I must explain that fish and chip suppers are very much a part of the culture of the North of England. We have fish and chips shops that open until quite late at night and the staff sprinkles them with salt and vinegar and then wrap them up in paper for you. I checked in the kitchen but no one was there and then when I went back into the healing room, the smell was stronger than ever. I was convinced that Lyn knew this lady because her presence was so compelling, but once again she said that she had no idea who it was. I asked if the fish and chips meant anything to her as they obviously held some significance. 'No, they mean nothing, Mick.' I told Lyn that only on rare occasions did I feel such a strong link as this lady was giving me and I felt certain that she must mean something to her and the smell remained throughout the healing. We talked about it afterwards and I told Lyn that I felt that this lady was really close to her, she would not leave and kept bringing the odour of the fish and chips to my senses but Lyn still denied knowing her.

The following day, around lunchtime at the clinic, a knock came to the door and it was Lyn, she was sobbing and extremely distressed, so much so that I left the client that I was treating and came out to see her. Between the sobs, she told me that after she left the clinic yesterday, she went to visit her mother. She arrived there about seven-thirty in the evening and the door was locked and there was no reply so she let herself into the house. She looked around the lounge and the kitchen but the house appeared empty so she started to go up the stairs. There the terrible sight

confronted her, her mother had hung herself from the landing and her face was blue. Lyn raced to the telephone to get the police and ambulance that came within seconds but it was too late, her mother had committed suicide. She was of course in a state of complete shock and the doctor was sent for to calm her down.
The next day, as she was in no state of mind to eat or cook, she took her children to the fish and chip shop for their lunch and it was while she was in there that it hit her.

On the Monday she had called at her mother's shop, which was in the centre of town and it was lunch-time. She had a quick chat with her as she was in a bit of a hurry, and then said that she must dash. As she got to the shop door, she turned to look at her mother who was having fish and chips for lunch and liked them covered in lots of vinegar. 'The vision of my mother stood before me, eating fish and chips, that is what you gave me yesterday Mick.' The poor lady was inconsolable.

She got the children their fish and chips and had run to see me. She knew now that it was her mother who came to her yesterday, the fish and chips had been her last meal.

When her mother left the shop, she called at a hardware store and bought a length of rope, intending to hang herself with it and the old lady had carried out her intentions.

How often do we not know of the emotions that our loved ones are feeling? Why did the old lady not share her despair; so often we miss the signals.

Lyn's husband Bob had totally disbelieved the story. They went out one day for a ride into the countryside sometime later and while in the car Bob began to sniff, 'I can smell fish and chips Lyn, with lots of vinegar on them, have you put some in the car for lunch?' 'It is my mother,' Lyn said. 'I was just thinking of her.' Several times after this she would smell it all over the house, in the bedroom and bathroom, everywhere and on Lyn's next visit for the healing, as soon as she entered the room the smell of fish and chips came with her.

We never really found out the reason why Lyn's mother had killed herself, but I feel that she thought that she had cancer, that is why she had taken her own life. On Lyn's next visit to the sanctuary she asked me if her mother was still around. I could not smell or sense anyone this time and said that probably her mother was doing some work in the spirit world. Lyn went home after the healing and Mavis asked me to go into the kitchen, there again was the smell of fish and chips with lots of vinegar and mum was still here. We said a little prayer for her.

I suppose that this story tells of the many ways that Spirit communicates with us and not always by visions of them or speaking to us. They also communicate using our fondest memories, a certain smell, maybe a perfume, coming into the room, or the smell of our favourite flowers. It could be a cigarette or pipe or maybe a cigar smell of the grandfather. I have known it to be apple blossom. I know a lady that gets, shall we say, 'a rural smell,' whenever a farmer friend of hers is around. Lyn's mother had brought this smell with her as it was the last moment that they shared here on Earth. Often, when you are sat quietly, thinking your thoughts, thinking of some past memory, Spirit will come, you may be thinking about a parent or a beloved grandparent, or even a precious child. If you cannot feel their presence then maybe if you just smell, you will know that they are around. Sit back and sense the air around you, for they are surely there. Just give it a try and send out your thoughts of love to them, they will be received wholeheartedly.

Positive Mental Attitude

Illness unfortunately has no regard for age or status and my mate Charlie had a stroke in his early fifties, which rendered him paralysed down one side. He told me that he had heard about a Methodist healer, who was due to visit our town and was really excited and placing high hopes on this man making him better. I told him to calm down, as the healing did not work in the way that he thought it did. I went along to the meeting with him but he came out of there despondent and depressed. He still had very bad sciatica and was completely paralysed down one side. He told me that he felt very low and said that he had nothing to live for. I had a little chat with him and said 'Listen Charlie, let's work at it, would you give me six months to help you to feel better about yourself?' he agreed but was not a happy man, he had hoped for instant results.

He started coming to the Sanctuary each week for physiotherapy and healing. I worked his arthritic limbs to get more movement and each time he was a little more mobile. I had an idea that I thought might restore Charlie's self-worth again, so I went down to his house to see him. When he came to the door I asked him to get in my car; he was going for a driving lesson. He was a bit annoyed with me. 'What are you talking about Mick, I can't drive like this.' I told him that I had one of those special wheels fitted to the steering wheel of my car; one that could be steered with one hand. I was going to get him driving again.

We went up to the racecourse and Charlie drove around and around. 'Mick, this is absolutely fantastic,' he told me and his face was lit up like a beacon. Quite a number of weeks passed by and very slowly Charlie got his confidence back. He was assessed on his driving skills and a police inspector went with him to purchase a new mini that was specially converted for his disability. He still came for the healing and I always knew when it was him, as I would hear the car screaming up the street at fifty miles per hour; he drove like a teenager. He would hit the brakes hard in my driveway and I always told him off.

Healing is about working on the whole person, taking a holistic approach and Charlie, as well as being physically capable again, needed to work on his self-belief. Believing in yourself and being positive is absolutely essential to your life, a positive mental attitude makes so much difference. Well-done Charlie.

Back Problems

Once we learn to trust in Spirit, simply to accept and to follow, they will guide us down all the pathways that we need.

I went one day to observe a Methodist minister and his healing work. There were lots of people who were gathered there singing hymns and saying prayers. Most of them had gone with ordinary, everyday problems. I was very interested in curing such conditions, as so many were suffering from them. I remember watching a chap with a trapped sciatic nerve who was writhing around in pain in his seat. He sat right on the edge of his chair and could not keep still. He hobbled up to the minister, who placed his hands upon his back but went back to his seat still in a great deal of pain. He did not seem to have any release from the pain. I prayed to God and asked God if I could cure everyday conditions, I wanted to treat people with migraines, nervous breakdowns, trauma, bulimia and anorexia; the list is endless, I wanted to be able to treat any and every condition.

I had seen the wonderful cancer cures, they were miraculous, but I wanted to treat people every day, for every condition. I did not want to be greedy. I told God that I would gladly give up the miracles, if I could treat the people all the time. I wanted to work for God every day.

I had at this time, been seeing people with back problems in my Sanctuary but I never had any positive results. Week after week people would come and say that they were no better, until I felt disheartened and also quite embarrassed. These people were coming to me, placing their trust in me and I could not help them.

I felt that God had let me down and that I would never be able to cure a bad back. I could just not do it.

After one particularly bad day, I came home and I thought to myself, that is it, no more, I will never attempt to treat a

back problem again, and completely resigned myself to the fact that this was an area where I had failed.
As I washed my hands ready for our evening meal an invalid car pulled up in the street and a chap got out and knocked on the door. He was quite a tall man and was holding himself up on two walking sticks. 'Are you Mr. McGuire?' he said quite gruffly, 'I wonder if you could help me please. You are my very last hope. I have been everywhere and I have seen everybody, but nobody can help me, please tell me that you will try.'

I asked him what his problem was and he said that he had a bad back. I remember shaking my head and thinking that I could not do anything for this gentleman but he was in so much pain that I felt reluctant to turn him away. I decided, against my better judgement, that I would take him inside and just go through the motions. I sat him on the chair and I placed my hands upon his back. He groaned loudly and tried to straighten himself. It appeared that something was happening, but I did not feel too optimistic. I did all of the things that I normally do and thought that he could now go on his way and he went to stand up and walk across the room. He bent down to pick up his walking sticks from the floor.

Then he gave out a loud shout and waved them in the air. He went around the room again throwing them on the floor and picking them up. I followed him with my hands on my head, 'Please, please be careful,' I begged him, 'Do not do anything drastic with your back.' He smiled and thanked me profusely, then he picked up his sticks and off he went, back to his little invalid car, he was smiling from one ear to the other.

From that day on, I have helped hundreds of people with back conditions; from the moment that I said that God had let me down, I have cured hundreds of backs.

Once again Spirit had heard my prayers, had heard my

thoughts and guided me down the right pathway. Working for God, doing the healing is my life and it is fantastic. I want to help mankind, through God, with all of its suffering, I could not have chosen a finer path.

The Healing Demonstration

I went to do a demonstration of the healing at a theatre in Derby and was billed as The Healerman. When I arrived the woman who worked behind the bar told me that she had a bad knee and asked if I could take a look at it. I gave her some healing on the knee before the show started and she went outside to telephone her boyfriend to tell him that her pain had gone. He did not believe her but she screeched at him, 'I am here now and he has just treated me, I am telling you, the pain in my knee has gone.' The woman could hardly believe it herself. The lighting technician then asked me to look at his bad back so I manipulated it for a short while and he too said that he felt much better. Mavis my assistant had come along to help me and my wife came to watch the demonstration.

Several people did different things on stage and then it came to my spot on the show. I thought that I would start with something simple like a bit of arthritis or spondylosis. I asked if there was anyone in the audience, who was suffering from a neck problem and probably thirty or forty people put up their hands. I felt drawn to an elderly lady who was sitting on the right hand side of the audience and invited her up onto the stage. Two people went to give her a hand, as she was badly crippled. It seemed to take an eternity for her to get up onto the stage. I held the microphone to her mouth and asked if she would like to tell me what her problems were. She said that she had bone cancer and that she had a plate in her hip and her leg. This lady had not been able to move her neck for years and was obviously very poorly. I felt at her neck but it was absolutely solid; it would not move to the left or the right, I could not rotate it in any direction.

I knew that I was in trouble, there was no way that I would be able to manipulate this neck so I went round to the back of her and put my hands upon her shoulders. To say that I was panicking was a complete understatement; here I was on the stage doing a healing demonstration and I had got before me a neck that I could not move. I knew that there was only one thing that I could do and that was to pray. I sent up a prayer to ask God what I should do, as I thought that I was going to look a fool. A voice came back which just said, 'Be honest.' Right then, I thought, this is what I must do. The voice repeated itself, 'Be honest, and tell the truth.'

I gave the woman a little bit of healing and gathered myself to tell the audience that I could not help this lady. I began. 'As you can see ladies and gentleman, this lady is a very, very sick,' and I put my hand on the top of her head to show them that there was no movement in her neck. I was just going to say what I was thinking when the lady's neck moved right under my hand. It moved to the left, to the right, backwards and forwards, it was perfect. I breathed a sigh of relief, 'As you can see ladies and gentleman, her neck is now completely free.' There was a huge gasp followed by rapturous applause and the woman began to cry. I was in a total state of shock. God had not let me down; He was right there beside me. Why had I doubted Him, O ye of little faith. Here I was once again letting myself down by doubting; doubting a God that had never let me down.

The manager then asked for volunteers to come up on to the stage and around twenty people came forward. They were all given a chair and I went up and down the line, holding their hands, praying for them to be well again. Mavis followed me down the line. I asked God for forgiveness for the people, for comfort for those who were bereaved. As I put my hands on the head of one young man, I felt him go. He was slipping down in the chair, so I shouted for my assistant Mavis to come and hold him. I carried on moving down the line but Mavis had to shout me back. Each person that I touched went unconscious. She shouted to me, 'Mick, he is unconscious.' 'I know that he is, that is why I am asking you to hold him.' I carried on moving down the line; some people asked for healing for cancer, some for pain relief, some for a prayer, each had their own needs.

I prayed for each one in their turn and eventually it was time for the end of my spot. It was the middle of the evening and was time for refreshments for the audience. I was to be followed on the stage by a psychic, who was to give messages out to the people.

The curtains closed to rapturous applause and we went off stage into the back room. The stage door had been left open and suddenly about thirty people came rushing in, all asking for healing. I was a bit overwhelmed at first but I asked for some chairs and started to go through each and every one of them. Mavis and I prayed for each one in their turn and administered the healing then the stage manager asked for the stage to be cleared for the show to continue. Nobody moved, everyone stated that they were not moving until I had seen them. He was not pleased at all but I just carried on.

We healed as many people as we could but then more and more people climbed up, everything was getting completely out of control. Finally there were about twenty people left and I knew that the show could not be held up anymore. I asked everyone if they would please come back to the dressing room, where I said prayers and began the healing again. Some people were grieving, some had lost their faith, some people had delved with Spirit, but found that it had not worked for them and they were afraid. I told them, whenever you are afraid, go straight to God, talk to Him and tell Him what is in your heart.

When I looked outside the door, there were people queuing up down the corridor and right to the outside. The stage manager was really annoyed now and told them that they must go back to their seats or leave. I felt honoured that all these people had faith in what I was doing but it was time for us to go. We had to rush, as the car park where we had parked closed its gates at eleven o'clock and it was about five minutes to go. I was wet through with sweat but what a wonderful, fulfilling evening it had been; there is nothing greater than working for God. We worked straight through without a drink or a break but I did not feel hunger or thirst, only elation. I felt drained and tired but very uplifted.

We talked over the events of the evening all the way home in the car; it was a tremendous night that we will never forget. I talked to my wife and Mavis of how once again I had doubted and God had stepped in to show me the way, to show me that while I put myself forward as His vessel, then He will be there to bring the healing. How often in life is it our own doubts that stop us from doing things. How often do we stop ourselves from starting something in the first place, by thinking that we are not capable; letting negativity take over before we even begin. What about all the people out there, who would love to be healers, who are healers, but believe that they cannot do it. I am telling you friends, all that you need is faith and love and God will do the rest.

Healing is the most simple and natural thing and no tools needed. Just sit someone down and place your hands upon their head and ask God to heal them; it is as simple and as easy as that.

God is there all of the time, not part of the time, He is all knowing and is listening to anyone and everyone; the love of God has no boundaries. He wants us all to heal, to help each other and to give love wherever we can. The most important thing that you must do during healing is to give of your love. This is the first and foremost rule. It is vitally important because it is what God wants us to do; it is love that holds all of the power.

Give it a try, and remember that healing can never harm; it is always for the good. Let us use the gifts that God has given us to the fullest extent for the benefit of all. Be aware not to make any promises about the outcome, for it is God that decides that; you and I are merely the channel. Just imagine what a wonderful place the world would be if we all gave each other a little healing. It would become the most natural thing to do. Just as it should be for it is as natural as breathing and comes from the highest source.

I am not telling anyone to ignore orthodox medicine but to combine it with the healing force, for God has also taught the minds of conventional medicine.

Healing has been with us since time began and we all do it without always being aware. We give words of kindness to a passer by, healing words; we give cuddles and hugs to our children, our animals and each other. Holding the hand of a sick person; the healing touch.

Take all of this a step further and consciously heal. Place your hands upon the head of someone, who is sick and give out your love or just even hold their hand and say a prayer for them. God will be there to assist you, have no doubt about that. Do not doubt that you can do this my friends, as to heal is as natural as the air that we breathe and it is simply a part of our being that we have allowed to be lost.

May God give you all the courage to have a first attempt, for it will be so wonderful that you will never look back.

The Faceless One:
A Great Teacher

One of my spirit guides is a man that I call 'The Faceless One'. He is a monk who dresses in a brown robe and I call him this because he has never allowed me to see his face. He has taken me on many journeys into the world of spirit; all of them for important lessons that I needed to learn. A very important thing for us all to learn is to face our fears; the fears that are borne for whatever illogical reason, that block our pathway to insight and truth. The Faceless One has taught me many things; things about the fears that I have hidden within myself. My monk is very small in stature but a great teacher. He waits for me in the hours of sleep, to begin the lessons that I need to learn in order for my healing to progress. He beckons to me to follow him and we go on to the other dimensions; to the realms of the spirit world. He has opened many doors for me and his power is great. I am very grateful for all the journeys that I have travelled as his companion. He usually appears to me at night at the end of my bed; but he never shows me his face, it is simply a shadow. I have complete faith that he will protect and take care of me. His wisdom is far greater than mine and I follow wherever he leads.

Everything is known in the spirit world; even things that we do not know about ourselves. My own fear regarding the healing was that I was afraid of women with mental illnesses; I was very afraid. It stemmed from something that happened in my childhood but I had buried it deep in my subconscious. I would certainly not be able to heal women with mental problems, as I was too frightened. This stemmed from the time, when I was fourteen years old and during lunchtime at school. In the evenings after four o'clock, I had a delivery round. I worked for the local grocery store and did deliveries for them on my pedal bike. I put the groceries in the basket at the front of my bike and drop them off at the customers' houses.

There was a house that I delivered to on a Friday evening. I carried the groceries down the yard and knocked on the door. They would ask me in and I would place the groceries on the kitchen table.

The door to their sitting room would usually be open and on the opposite wall of the sitting room, above the fireplace, was a mirror. There was a young woman, who looked at me through this mirror. She would lock her eyes on to me and never smiled or changed her expression, just stared in a wild sort of manner. I tried to avert my eyes but I never could and even though I was frightened, I still had to look to see if she was there. As soon as I saw her, I was terrified and got out of the house as quickly as I could. A young boy's mind is very impressionable. Her parents always gave me a rather generous tip of one shilling but quite honestly I would have preferred to miss out on the money than have to go into that house. The girl's face would stay with me when I left. I could still see her in my mind's eye, staring at me with that awful haunted look in her eyes. I feel sure that this was where my fear of mental illness stemmed from. It was an important lesson that I was to learn this night and would enable me to go forward with the healing work.

I remember that I was really, really tired. I had been out healing almost every night and my family were complaining that I was never at home and said that they would like to have some time with me. It was very hard to say no to my patients as there were so many, who were ill and in need of the healing. I dragged my body heavily up the stairs; telling myself that I must lighten my workload and make more time for the family. The lovely warmth of the room and my big comfortable bed felt like heaven and I soon drifted off into a deep sleep The Faceless One was there to greet me.

I had been working all day but now my work was to begin again. He came beside me as usual and beckoned for me to follow him. He took me to a room, an empty room with a large imposing door. He went then and I was alone. As I stood there, all sorts of thoughts were going around in my head; my stomach was churning and I felt sweaty and nervous. I knew that there was no choice in the matter; the door must be opened and I knew that behind the door was something that I needed to learn. I hesitated some more and offered a prayer for guidance. What was waiting for me? My hands were slippery with sweat, as I reached to turn the handle. I pushed the door open quickly, while I had the courage. I recoiled in horror at the sight that was before me and pressed my back hard against the wall; my outstretched arms holding on to the bricks to steady myself. Every vein in my body was filled with an ice-cold terror.

At this point I started to gasp for breath and was pouring with a fear-induced sweat. I closed my eyes tightly and prayed, I prayed that when I opened them again, that I would be back in my own bed, safe. I remember saying to myself, 'my God, my God what am I to do.' In the middle of the room were the head and torso of a woman. She looked blind and her face held the same wild and contorted expression that I had seen in that mirror many years ago. It obviously reflected her poor ravaged mind and I could not cope with this. I steeled myself to do something. She was screeching really loudly and flailing her arms around.

My thought processes came to an abrupt halt and I seemed to be frozen in time. I called out to her and then shouted but did not get any response. She carried on screeching and then it occurred to me that she was also deaf but I was too afraid at this point to feel any compassion for this poor creature. She shuffled herself forward and grasped at my leg, frantically trying to claw her way up to my face. I can only equate the feeling to when someone who is arachnophobic has a huge spider on their face, the sheer mind numbing terror. I was just enveloped in a blanket of fear.

She was blind and deaf and I could not communicate with her; how was I supposed to reach this woman? Keeping my eyes tightly shut, I tentatively reached out and placed one of my hands on the top of her head and mentally sent her my love. My arm shook with fear and she pulled at my legs, until I went down to the floor in a heap and she fell down with me.

I wrapped my arms tightly around her and sent her waves of love and placed both of my hands on her head and again sent her love; through my hands, through the healing. Gradually, slowly, she loosened the grasp on my leg and then went completely quiet.

We lay silently together on the floor; the screeching had stopped and she was no longer flailing around. Her head went onto my chest and I continued to heal her and give her my love. I did not feel afraid anymore and she seemed at last to find peace.

A sense of calm came into the room and I closed my eyes and prayed for her. I was not frightened anymore and I prayed that she would be given peace and then opened my eyes. I realised at this point that she was simply a woman. How afraid she must have been, unable to see or hear and having no legs to move around properly. Her only feeling, her only sense, was that of confusion and fear. Why are we so afraid of something that is different to us? I felt overcome with sorrow for her and felt shame that I had not seen her as a person but had only thought of myself. I realised that my previous moments of agony were what this poor tortured soul had suffered every day. Not only suffering from all her afflictions, but also rejected by people and denied of their love. Why can we not see that people like her need our love more than anyone else. They need a special kind of love and 'there but for the grace of God go I.'

This was a crucial lesson for me as healing is about many things. It is about using all of our senses; about having the insight to put ourselves in another person's shoes. What would we expect from society had we been in the position of this woman and what would we have actually received? Society should assess itself on how the weakest are cared for. If our vulnerable are loved and cared for, then we have a good world to live in. We could come back the weakest in another lifetime.

I now come to realise that literally millions of people suffer from mental illness; I think that maybe every one of us has suffered at some point in our lives. Life can be very hard and cruel and we need to help each other through it. We can only help the world to deal with mental illness by bringing it out, no shame attached, just like a broken leg, so that people who are suffering can go forward. We all must face our fears and look at how they hinder us or our dealings with others. We need to put down the barriers that we carry around with us every day and give our love to the people, whoever they are and whatever they suffer from.

Mental Illness

The secretary from the local psychiatric hospital rang me to see if it were possible to bring one of their patients to see me. The psychiatrist, who had been treating this lady said that she was not responding to any of the treatments and the doctors felt that they could not make her any better and wondered if there were anything I could do. She asked if I would mind if the minister came along too and I told them that was fine and made an appointment to see her later in the day. When the woman came in, she didn't look at me; her head was bowed down and she looked in a traumatised state. She sat on the massage table rocking backwards and forwards. I asked her to lie down and gently began to stretch and manipulate her neck and I then manipulated all of her joints. She turned over and I put the massage machines on her back. I noticed the secretary and the minister looking at me and knew that they were wondering what on earth I was doing. This lady had come to me for mental health problems not physical ones. The mind and body work together; when one is not in harmony then neither is the other. The physiotherapy relaxes the muscles and settles the person down in readiness for the healing.

I turned the lights down low and began to administer the healing; she now started to look more calm and peaceful. When the healing was over, I turned to put the lights back on, when the lady jumped off the table and ran towards me to give me a hug. 'That was absolutely beautiful,' she said and her face was vibrant and smiling. The minister and the secretary were sitting with their mouths open. She walked out of the Sanctuary a different person; her body language so totally different. She strode across the room with her head held high. The secretary asked me how much she owed me and I told her that it was okay but to please let me know how the lady progressed.

Much to my surprise, I received a telephone call the next day to tell me that the lady wanted to go home. The secretary was amazed at this, as the patient had become increasingly dependant upon the psychiatric ward over the years and was slowly becoming more and more institutionalised before the healing. They assured me that they would monitor the situation for quite a while but felt confident that she would now be able to manage on her own. I never get over the feeling of euphoria, when someone is so much better and I never forget to give thanks to God, for it is He who gives the healing. I am merely the channel.

Physical Medium

Many years ago, during the peak of my development, I was made President of the Spiritualist Church in Doncaster. I took a group of people on a special evening out to a physical phenomena circle in Preston. Our instructions beforehand were that we must be bathed, have nothing to eat but may have a drink of tea or water; in other words, we must be cleansed. When we arrived at our destination we were then taken somewhere else for the venue. It was a sealed room with no doors or windows and it held a black, curtained chamber for the medium.

There were twelve of us in all, six from my group and six from the Preston circle. The opening prayer was said and we started to sing some old fashioned songs. Old English songs such as 'Roll Out the Barrel' and 'My Old Man's a Dustman' were sung.
It was a lovely start and the singing was done boisterously and lifted up the room.

On the floor was a trumpet, which had been painted with illuminous paint. At the side of it was a plaque, a small flat piece of wood that had also been covered with the illuminous paint. We sang for about ten to fifteen minutes and then the lights were put out and the room was in total darkness. It was completely black with not a flicker of light. The trumpet moved up into the air and was floating around making noises just as if someone was trying to speak through it and tapped some people on the nose. The plaque started to circle the room, first of all very slowly but then whizzing around at enormous speed; it flew around and around and finally stopped at me, Mick.

I watched in utter amazement as a child's hand crawled over it. It crawled over the plaque on to my hand and I felt around it to see if there were any strings attached to it. In other words, I wanted to see if it was a trick but I found nothing. I couldn't believe what I was seeing.

The medium, who was male, came out from behind a

curtain and had ectoplasm coming out of his mouth; it went right down to the floor. He started to speak and asked me if I would like to touch the ectoplasm. I was very intrigued and said that, yes, I would. It felt very dry and reminded me of the consistency of sacking cloth. It was not at all wet, as I had expected it to be. He lifted the ectoplasm and placed it on my lap and said that one day I would be a physical medium, as he was.

After that there were several messages passed on to people from the spirit world and then the meeting was closed with prayers and flowers were thrown on to the floor.

After the circle ended, the sitters got together for light refreshments and to chat. They were all asked to decide whether they thought that the medium was true or fraudulent. It was at this point that I found out that nobody else in the group had heard the conversation between the medium and myself. He had spoken quite clearly to me, not in a whisper but a normal voice and it sounded as clear as a bell to me. What a revelation, to become a physical medium; this step forward really excited me and I still wait patiently for that day to come.

A Tortured Soul

Ted was my wife's uncle, a good man whom I liked very much. He was a tall, handsome chap who was kind and sensitive and all of his family adored him. He enjoyed the simple things in life; an occasional drink, a bet on the horses and going out in the car with his wife and daughters. Ted worked for the National Coal Board and his work took him to various collieries in the South Yorkshire area.

One evening when he was coming home from work, an elderly lady stepped out in front of his car, there was nothing that Ted could do; he was unable to stop in time. The old lady was taken to the hospital, where before her injuries healed, she died of pneumonia. Ted was devastated; this gentle, sensitive man could not cope with the fact that he had taken a life. It was a tragic accident and was certainly not his fault. He was always a steady and observant driver but Ted could not accept this and was absolutely consumed with guilt, questioning himself over and over if there was something that he could have done to avoid what happened.

He went to work one morning at his local colliery and made an excuse to go into the cage alone, where he opened the cage door and fell to his death down the pit shaft. His family were heartbroken, including my wife and could not understand why this dear man had done such a thing. No one realised the extent of the mental anguish that Ted was going through.

Shortly after the funeral one of his daughters contacted me, as she was worried about her dad; about where he had gone. She could not get it out of her mind and was desperate to know that he was safe. I told her to go home and to pray for him, to pray every day and I would do my best to seek help from Spirit to find Ted. Before I drifted off to sleep I said a prayer for him asking my spirit friends if they could help me to find him.

During my sleep, my guide, The Faceless One, came and

beckoned me to follow. We went into the mouth of a cave and kept on going down deeper and deeper, through the labyrinths and down into the darkest depths. The vibrations down there were very unpleasant; it was not a nice place to be. When we reached the bottom I saw a man in front of me, he was facing the wall and it was Ted. I jumped up and down; I was so pleased that I had found him. I went over to him and put my hand upon his shoulder but there was no response. Ted did not even flinch; it was just like touching a piece of stone. I turned to The Faceless One for help, but he beckoned to me that we must leave.

I didn't want to go. I had found Ted and I wanted to rescue him. I did not want to leave him in this place of darkness. Why wasn't I able to reach him? The Faceless One beckoned again, this time turning away to leave. I knew that I must follow him; his wisdom was far greater than mine and he would never steer me wrong. I woke up the next morning but was not happy because I knew that Ted had decided his own fate. In the world of Spirit we are not punished, for it is a place of pure love but our own soul decides what we feel that we deserve. Ted did not deserve this but he had decided that he did; it was a terrible accident and I felt such sorrow for this kind man.

I thought that when I came home from work that I would go into meditation to see if I could find an answer. During my meditation the answer came to me. The old lady, she could save him, her forgiveness would release his soul and with the help of my wonderful guides I would try to find her. That night I prayed hard that the old lady could be found and The Faceless One turned up at my bedside accompanied by the old lady God Bless them. She had come to help bless her; The Faceless One had found her.

We set off on our journey once again, down through the entrance of the cave into the dark labyrinths. Once again going down into the depths until we reached the place where dear Ted was, still facing the wall. I stood to one side as the old lady went towards him. She put her hand on his right shoulder and Ted turned around to look at her. She put out her arms to him and Ted rose to his feet and she embraced him; she loved and forgave him. When we came out of the cave, the old lady, Ted and The Faceless One all turned and walked towards a stile, where they crossed over into the most beautiful light. My guide lifted his hand to me, I could go no further, it was not my time. Ted's soul had been taken to the light but my Earthly work was not over. This was only a grain of sand within the sands of time. I waited for them all to turn and acknowledge me, but they did not, they continued walking into the light.

There are no judge and jury, when we pass over to the other side of life; we judge ourselves, for no one is a harsher judge. Our own spirit knows everything that has happened in our lives and we must try to do our best here, while we are on the Earth plane and to seek forgiveness and re-instate the bonds of love wherever it is necessary.

Sometimes in life, we make judgements about ourselves that are borne of guilt and these judgements are not necessarily correct. We must remember that guilt can be a very negative emotion as sometimes things that happen in life are not our fault. We must never look backwards in life; we must always go forward. Do not dwell on things that have happened in the past, for these are all your lessons. We are sent here for our souls to learn; to learn love and forgiveness, compassion and joy. We have to go through the full spectrum of emotions and come out stronger at the other side. We need to pass over into the spirit world with a loving and learned heart, pray every day my friends for yourself and those around you.

God Bless you, Ted dear friend.

The Garden of Love

This is the story of Jane Reid, a very special story about someone who was very dear to my heart. I had lots of miracles with the healing, the story of Peter and of Hilda the lady with all the cancerous growths. I had so many successes and my healing guides were so powerful that I felt that I could cure almost anything.

Jane was a colleague of mine at the ICI plant and her husband Bob worked there too; both were great friends of mine. She was a beautiful young lady, very bouncy and bubbly and always pleasant to everyone but Jane developed cancer.

I met her first of all at the church, when she first found out that she was ill she started to come to church and just like my friend Billy Dutton, she said that it was like going home. She told me that she felt that here in the church, her spiritual needs were being met. Although I got to know them both very well I did not know at the time that this was to be the start of a very spiritual relationship with the two of them.

Jane came first to my little garage for the healing but she was not getting any better. The hospital was removing tumours from her all of the time, usually by local anaesthetic. I remember driving along in my car and getting pain and this always coincided with the time that Jane was having the local anaesthetic for the tumour removal; we seemed to be very connected spiritually. I used to pick up on her thoughts and fears each week, when she came to the Sanctuary. One particular night when she came to me, she was so ill that she had hit two cars while driving here and arrived in a really distressed state. As time went by she became more and more poorly, until eventually she could no longer get to the Sanctuary and it was then that I went to their home to treat her.

One evening, when I arrived there, I found Bob looked really tired and drained, the strain of caring for Jane, although he did it with all his heart and soul, was beginning to show. I told him to go out for a short while, just to go and have a break somewhere and told him that I would stay until he came back and that Jane would be quite safe with me, I would call him if anything happened. He was reluctant to go but finally relented and went out for an hour or so.

After he had gone I began with the healing, it was beautiful healing but shortly afterwards Jane asked me if I would mind putting her on the commode. I said that of course I would not and gently lifted her now extremely frail body onto it, I left her in private for a little while. She called to me that she could not do anything and could I put her back into the bed but as I went to put her back in bed everything came away from her. She was very, very embarrassed. I told Jane it was not a problem and that she must not worry herself about it.

I went to get a bowl of water and I gently cleaned Jane up first, made her comfortable and gave her some fresh clothing. I then stripped the bed and put clean linen on and got some more water and disinfectant for the carpet. I didn't feel embarrassed about it at all; it is all part of the caring process, all our bodies function in the same way.

Bob came back about an hour or so later and started to tell me that Jane had been ill for over a year now and as he had not been able to work they were really struggling financially. He did not say this where Jane could hear of course. He loved her very much and would have done anything for her. He told me that his car was a problem because it was too expensive for him to run. It was quite a new car, newer than my car but it had a large engine and the petrol and running costs were high. He said that he would just have to sell it and manage without a car. My car at that time was a Shooting Brake, I had just had it re-sprayed and some minor jobs done on it. It was a lower engine than Bob's car was and he asked me if I would do him a straight swap. I knew that he was really struggling financially and that if I didn't swap him he would not be able to keep a car on the road. I agreed and said that if we did this, I must give him five hundred pounds as well, because his car was not as old as mine. He said no but I told him that, if he did not accept the money as well, then the deal was off. I did not have five hundred pounds at that time but I knew that his need was greater than mine, so I borrowed it from the bank and we swapped cars. I felt that it was a small thing to do for such lovely people.

Jane was becoming increasingly poorly and I knew that her time was very close; I went out almost every night to see her. I was getting ready to go and see her one night when my wife came to talk to me. She told me that I had got a wife and family of my own and did I not think that they needed some of my time. She said that I had been going out to do healing night after night and that the family never saw me. She wanted me to spend some time with them. She had a point; I had been coming in from work every night and going straight out to do the healing. I was so wrapped up in my work that I did not think about those at home.

I rang Billy Dutton and asked if he would go out to see Jane for me. He had helped me to heal Jane in the Sanctuary and she knew him very well. Billy rang me later to say that Jane's time was very near, she could hardly speak and had kept asking for me. Jane passed away that night. I was so upset that I had not been to see her on the last night of her life. I felt that she would have needed the spiritual upliftment and guidance. I said prayers for her but felt extremely sad and guilty.

The following day, I was on day shift at work, 6.00 a.m. until 2.00 p.m. and got home about 2.30 p.m. and my wife was still at work. I felt really tired and lay down on the settee in the living room for a rest.

Within a few moments I was asleep and found myself

walking towards a large house. Outside the gate of the house was a nurse who said to me 'You have come to see Jane.' I said 'Yes I have, I am very concerned about her, how is she?' She assured me that she was fine. I did not believe this and asked her how could she be fine, she weighed less than six stones, had lost all of her hair and was ravaged with cancer. I told her that yesterday she was bedridden so how can she be fine today. She repeated once again that Jane was fine and said 'If you go down the side of the house, you will be able to see her.' I opened the gate and ran down the path at the side of the house as fast as I could. I will never forget what I saw that day, it was so-so beautiful, it reminded me of Dorothy in the Wizard of Oz.

All the colours took my breath away; they were more vivid than I had ever seen. There were big beautiful trees and green, green grass. All types of flowers, exotic and colourful, were in this garden and people were everywhere. Lots and lots of people, of all ages, children, elderly and teenagers, middle-aged. They were all mixing together and running about and there were birds and fishponds and animals.

Everybody seemed to be enjoying themselves, all content and happy. All of a sudden I saw Jane, not the Jane that I had healed the week before, not the Jane ravaged with cancer, she was back to the beautiful, full, able-bodied person that I had known a long time ago. Her lovely long hair was blowing in the breeze and she was smiling and shouting my name and running towards me. I put my arms out to her and cuddled her. She held on to me and said that it was lovely to see me. We hugged each other for a few minutes and then two people in white coats came up and told her that she must come now.

They told me that I must stand back and Jane was a bit upset, she wanted to carry on hugging me. They turned to me, 'You now must go, it is time.' I remember her face staring at me; a huge part of me wanted to stay with her and it was very difficult to take it all in. I knew that I had to go back. I had been given the privilege of seeing Jane on the other side. I turned to walk out, down the side of the house and back to the gate and once I went through the gate, I was awake and back on the settee.

I had been taken to the spirit world, because I had been so upset about Jane. I felt heartbroken, because I was not there when she needed me. I asked myself if it would have made a difference to her death as people told me that I had failed with her, because she died and I did not make her better.

I now know that I did not fail with Jane at all. She was safe and well; she was one of my greatest successes and I had been taken to the spirit world to see that. It was her time to go and we cannot change that. We are not always healing the body; people do not always get better, either physically or mentally. Sometimes the healing is a far, far greater thing. It is a spiritual thing; it is a healing of the soul.

We do not always save the material, the physical, but strengthen the spirit. Jane was given help and strength; even in life her spirit became stronger, in spite of her physical condition. The strength helped her to cope in her last hours and she was not afraid of death, I did not let her down, because it was her time to go.

The garden in the spiritual world, that was God's garden and nothing like it will ever be seen here on Earth. People go there to rest and recuperate, when they have died of severe illness or have died in pain, they are cared for there until they are ready and well enough to move on. It is a hard lesson for all healers that we are not always able to save the material, the physical but through the healing we know that we can never, ever fail.

When you administer healing, you cannot fail, because you are touching the soul of that person and the soul is the most important thing because it is eternal. It is so very important to touch the soul, to heal the soul, because that soul has an eternal life, not a short one as the material body does, the soul has to go on, on its eternal journey. The people in God's kingdom care deeply about us and they help us in the journey of our souls whenever they can. Jane had gone to God's garden to recuperate, to regain her energies and to understand the new world that she had gone into. There were people there to guide and to help her; her loved ones and animals.

I cannot tell you how wonderful is God's garden. It inspired me to write a small poem dedicated to her called the Garden of Love. Once again I had been given the privilege of going into the spirit realms, to see where we go, when our time on this Earth ends. We are taught to fear death and that it is the end of everything but this is not true. Our bodies may be done with but the spirit inside us goes on to the next dimension, back to where it came from, to the love and care of God. I will never forget the sunshine and the colours in that garden and the happiness radiating from everyone there; it was utterly peaceful and perfect. They say that we only dream in black and white but I know that this was not a dream. This was another lesson for my spiritual enlightenment, to meet Jane on the other side of life when I was not there, when her physical body died but I was given the privilege of seeing that her spirit was safe, that it had gone on to continue its journey. My poem 'The garden of love' is dedicated to Jane.

The Garden of Love

Let us walk into The Garden of Love
Where the sun shines so brightly above
Where there are young folk and old folk
and animals too
And fish in a pond so lovely to view
It's peaceful and restful to sit for a while
In His wonderful Garden of Love
So God will draw close to your inner thoughts
His beauty and love he will bring
To soothe all the wounds of material life
Then for you the birds will sing
In His wonderful Garden of Love
Yes, that's what awaits us if we just sit and think
Of the world that He gave us and the beauty within
So sit for a while, let your thoughts go away
In His wonderful Garden of Love

Lost Soul

This is the story of Jane's husband, Bob Reid. I was working in my clinic in Doncaster, the clinic where I work now and it was a really busy day, the clinic was always full, people coming and going all of the time. We worked each day from early morning sometimes until seven in the evening and I was just about to close so I went around the rooms switching everything off. It was a Wednesday evening and we had finished a little earlier that day, it was about six-thirty, all of the girls had gone and I picked up my briefcase to leave. I glanced out of the window and there seemed to be a fog coming in, the street was uncannily quiet too, there was usually a hectic stream of traffic up and down, but tonight there was not a car in sight. I couldn't see any people either; I thought perhaps that everyone had gone home early because the weather was quite bad. I locked the clinic door and crossed over the road to my car and as I crossed I could see a figure standing beside the car but I could not make out who it was. As I got a bit nearer I realised it was Bob Reid.

It was several years after Jane's death and Bob had now re-married, I think that this was his third wife. When Jane and Bob had been together, before she had got the cancer, they adopted two children; I knew that they would have been about three or four years old now. I had never heard anything about them since Jane's death and I shouted over to him. 'Is that you Bob?' he looked a bit lost but he shouted, 'Who is it?' 'It's me Mick, Mick McGuire.' 'Of course it is Mick, how are you?' I told him that I was fine and asked how he was. He was very upset; there were tears in his eyes.

'I have just lost my wife Mick.' 'Oh no Bob, not another.' It was enough for any man to lose one wife, but he had lost three. 'I am so, so sorry Bob.' I asked him how he had coped and said that it was terrible to lose one wife, but three was unthinkable. He just shook his head so I tried to change the subject and asked how the children were. He said that they were growing up now and that they were doing just fine. I was pleased to hear that and I know that Jane would have been watching over them from the spirit world. He told me that he was living just down the road and said that he lived at Number One, Beckett Road and would I like to go and have tea with him sometime. I told him that it would be great to get together and talk about old times and that I would certainly take him up on his offer of tea.

All the time that I was stood talking to Bob I could not get out of my mind the peculiar feeling in the street that night, a sort of eeriness in the atmosphere. There was a strange mist hung around and a distinct lack of people and traffic. I shook Bob's hand and told him how sorry that I was to meet him under such circumstances. I said that I had to dash as I needed to get home but I would ring him to arrange to go for tea. He walked away really slowly looking lonely and dejected. I made a mental note in the car on the way home to keep my promise of going to meet him.

The following Friday while I was working in the Sanctuary one of my old work colleagues came in for some treatment. We were chatting and he said to me, 'It is a shame about Bob Reid isn't it Mick.' I agreed that it was terrible; I said that I could not believe that he had lost his third wife. 'No, I am not talking about that Mick,' he said. 'Bob had a car crash on Tuesday afternoon, his car hit a tree, he was killed instantly.' I said that I thought that he must have got his facts wrong, as I had spoken to Bob on Wednesday evening. I said that surely he must have got the dates wrong, but he assured me that he had not.

I knew at that moment that Bob had come to me when he passed over, I also knew that Bob did not realise where he was and came to me for guidance. I could not quite grasp that he had gone but I was sure that he was okay now in the spirit world and that he would be with Jane again or maybe one of his other wives. When you go over to the spirit world you can go where you want to go you can be with the people that you want to be with. If you have not been happy with the people in your life here on the material plane, then you may wish to move on in spirit and take a different path. The people who are in your life now may simply be with you for you to learn something from them. When you decide to take the spiritual path, God may ask you to do many things, things that you do not understand. We do not need to understand, but just to trust and accept everything that comes our way. We need to trust that the higher realms know much more than we and they are able to see the bigger scheme of things.

We are all here on Earth on a path of learning, a path to make our souls wiser. A path of progression, that when we once again enter the spirit realms, that we have learned much about ourselves and the people who share our lifetime.

Communicating with spirit is a communication through thought so it is important that our thoughts are good and right, because they are heeded in the higher realms, where everything is known. It is important to pray for ourselves and others as those thoughts go out there into the universe. It is important that our thoughts are of love and harmony, sow your seeds with love and you will reap the harvest of contentment and peace. Thoughts of love and goodness come back to the person one hundred fold. Do not send out bad thoughts to your enemies, wish them light and love. When we send out thoughts of hatred and revenge into the atmosphere, they cause havoc and eventually return, with more force than they went, to the person who sent them. If other people are treating you badly, pray for them to see the error of their ways. God bless you Bob as you go ever forward on your journey my friend.

The Disciples: Believe in yourself

This story is about a young boy of around 12 years old, who was brought for healing to my Sanctuary. His father carried the little lad in; his body was curled up tightly in a ball and he was unable to straighten any of his limbs and was rigid with pain. He laid him with great care onto my couch and placed him on his side. I talked to him for a little while then turned on the music and laid my hands upon him. I knew almost immediately that I would not be able to cure this child. I could not give him any physiotherapy, as he was too poorly, so I prayed deeply for him. I carried on with the healing to try and ease his suffering and he came to me for treatment on a regular basis but each time he left I felt very frustrated at the fact that I could do nothing for him.

Why could I cure people who were elderly and had experienced some life but not this poor young boy? I asked Spirit for their help, even though he received a great deal of peace from the healing, I wanted to do more.

It was in a despondent state that I retired to bed that night and during my deep sleep Spirit took me to a really hot, dry country. I got the feeling that it was Egypt or somewhere like that; it was very sandy and dusty. I was in the middle of a village and right in the centre was a well, which seemed to be the focal point where everyone gathered; people were going backwards and forwards to fetch water. I sat and observed all the activity from a bench at the side and the young boy who was ill was sat beside me. I approached one of the men, who was stood at the well and asked him why he was waiting there, because I did not know why I was there myself. He said that he had been told that two disciples were coming into town that day, two very special people.

A shiver of excitement went down my spine; now I knew why I was taken there, someone far greater than I would heal the boy. I waited for a while and heard people say that they would soon be there; they had heard that they were not very far away. When they arrived, the two were quite different in stature, one being really tall and the other quite small. Their clothes were very basic they were dressed in robes that were made of sackcloth and on their feet were sandals. They had a sort of leather emblem around their necks.

The two men went to the well for a drink and I felt that I must approach them with the needs of the boy. I noticed that the small one had really fat fingers. I approached them rather cautiously, 'I must speak to you,' I told them in an urgent voice, 'I need help, I cannot heal this boy, he is only over there, please can you help me?' I pointed to him and fully expected them to go straight over but their reaction was not what I expected.

They told me quietly but firmly, 'No,' they said that they did not need to, that I could heal him myself. I was shocked when they said this. This was not the reply that I had anticipated, and I came here because I could not make him better. They told me to have faith and placed a blessing upon the two of us.

When I woke up I felt a little different; stronger and more positive somehow. I carried on seeing the young man once a week for healing but unfortunately he died. It was his time to go and the healing helped him to pass comfortably. This was another lesson for me, to have faith in myself but not to be frustrated at the outcome. It is for God to decide when it is the time for someone to pass, not I. Many healers must feel inadequate if someone dies, but they are doing God's work and must feel worthy. As the lamp will not work without the electricity, so the healer cannot work without God. We are merely the lamps and God is the source of the power. It is He who chooses, who will survive or not.

I carried on doing my healing with a different kind of hope and I realise now that the child received comfort, peace and spiritual upliftment. I also realise that we must have the utmost faith in our ability to heal and to continue whatever happens, for Spirit will never desert us. So I say to all those out there who are giving healing, do not distress yourself if the outcome is that the person passes over, by administering the healing you will have helped their spirit to pass comfortably.

The Young Boy

As my psychic work progressed, alongside the healing, I have been called out on numerous occasions to deal with unusual happenings. Some of these have been very distressing, both for the people surrounding them and myself. At the church my aunt and uncle, Doris and Norman, tutored me. Doris was a very proficient psychic and Norman a healer. They worked devotedly for the church for many years and my aunt went out on occasions to places that were haunted. People rang her not knowing what to do and asked for her help. She rang me one day to ask if I would take on a particular haunting that she could not deal with and said that it seemed a bad one. She passed on all of the details, saying that the woman had a nervous breakdown because of the haunting and her husband had not been able to work for several weeks. It had got to the point where the council were having to re-house them.

She went on to tell me that the couple had two sons and they went out every evening and left the boys alone, even though the children were quite young. When they returned the children went off to bed and then the noises would start. The mother went into the kitchen to make a cup of coffee only to find everything in chaos. The table and chairs were turned upside down and the crockery smashed all over the floor.

She went from there and heard a light bulb being smashed against the wall but when she checked on the children they were always asleep, quite unaware of all the happenings. The woman then went into her bedroom to find that all the things from her dressing table were lying in disarray all over the floor. It had been going on for several months now and the man and woman were at the end of their tether.

I decided that I would go and see this for myself and my aunt and uncle asked if they could come along with me, so the three of us went at about ten-thirty one evening. The mother invited us to sit down and began shakily to tell the story. She said that it always started, when the fire was beginning to die down at the end of the day. A cold draught would come around their legs, making them shiver and this always happened about eleven-thirty each evening. First the cold then the smashing of the lights and finally all the furniture being tipped up.

I turned on the recording equipment that I had taken with me and we all sat quietly waiting, it was almost eleven-thirty and the children were tucked up safely in bed. We waited a while but nothing happened; midnight arrived and there was still no movement. I asked if they were sure that it was at the same time every night and they seemed a little perplexed; they couldn't understand why nothing was happening and assured me quite adamantly that it happened in the house at the same time every night. I explained that it maybe was the influence of psychic people being there that had stopped it but then I heard someone walking around upstairs. I asked the woman if she would go upstairs and tell the children that they must not get out of bed. She ran upstairs and returned to say that they were both fast asleep and as soon as she came back downstairs the footsteps on the ceiling started again.

I asked her once again if she would mind checking the children and she came down once again and said that they were both sleeping. I meditated for a little while, asking my spirit guides to help me. The thought came and I asked the lady if she would bring her eldest son downstairs to talk to me.

'What do you want him for?' she asked crossly. 'I am not waking him up, he is fast asleep.' 'Please do as I ask,' I had to insist. He was about eight years old and was rubbing his eyes as he came down the stairs; he seemed to be half-asleep. I sat him on the chair and put my hands on his head and he carried on sleeping. I put my mouth close to his ear and whispered to him, 'What do you think that you are doing son, why are you smashing the light bulbs and turning everything upside down in the kitchen and bedroom?'

He pretended that he was still sleeping and that he could not hear me. I told him that he must stop doing this as he was terrifying his mother. I told him that if he stopped doing this immediately then nothing else would be said on the matter and everything would be all right. He didn't give me a response but his parents did not look very pleased and glared at me, shaking their heads. His mother picked him up and took him back to his bed. Two minutes later there was a loud bang and the sound of glass smashing and this time I ran up the stairs, I was going to get to the bottom of this. The boy's bedroom had two single beds; one at either side of the room and the broken light bulb was on the bedroom floor.

I placed myself between the two of them and stood there really still for about ten minutes. The eldest boy turned over and opened his eyes. 'Who are you?' he said looking startled, I bent over the bed and said to him in a low tone, ' I think that you know who I am, if you have a problem son and you want to talk to me about it then I am here to listen. You have caused your mother to have a nervous breakdown and you have made it so that your father cannot go to work and leave her alone. This is a very dangerous game that you are playing.' He yawned with a little too much emphasis but kept his eyes firmly shut.

I knew now that this was not a haunting; this was a disturbed little lad. I left the bedroom door open and went out on to the landing outside and stood there for what seemed a while and was beginning to think that the child had actually gone off to sleep but I stayed silent. The eldest child then asked the youngest in a whispered tone if he was awake. 'Yes I am, and I saw you throw the light bulb at the wall.' That was all the confirmation that I needed so I went down stairs to tell the boys' parents what had really been happening.

Their house was not haunted; it was their eldest son doing all of these things. I felt quite proud of myself, I suppose it was my ego thinking that I was Sherlock Holmes getting to the bottom of the mystery. I felt uplifted when it was time to go, thinking that I had solved their problem successfully. I shook the hand of the lady and gentleman and said that I hoped that they were feeling so much better now and that things would improve.

'I feel terrible,' the mother said looking really angry, 'I have a real problem on my hands now and there is nothing that you can do about it.' It was by now the early hours of the morning and I was tired and weary, it had been a very long evening and the woman's response really deflated me. I had done my best to help her but she was not at all pleased with the outcome so I decided to go home, because I still had to get up for work the next morning.

It turned out not to be a haunting after all and what I had noticed when I was leaving was that on the side table in the living room was a book about the great psychic, Doris Stokes. It struck me then that the child had probably read some of the book and had taken his ideas from there. He decided that as he was not getting any attention that he would make things happen for himself. He had carried it on too far until it went way beyond the initial joke.

I felt satisfied then that I had sorted their problem out but it was at a much later time, when sat pondering that I realised that I had not completed my job properly with the boys. It was many years later, after I had completed several courses on counselling skills, that I realised how much more I should have helped those boys. It turned out that the wife and the boys' father had recently split up and she had taken on a new partner. Although the boys were very young, the couple were going off every evening to the local pub and leaving them alone, so the children were feeling unloved and neglected with their dad having gone and mum having a new man in her life. This was the young lad's way of seeking some attention.

I realise now, since completing the counselling courses, how much more I should have said to those parents, most certainly about leaving the children alone in the house but also about the boys' feelings of neglect and insecurity; the children needed to feel loved and safe.

Unfortunately we can only use the skills that we have at the time in any given situation. It goes to show that things are not always what they seem, sometimes Spirit may be blamed for things that are nothing to do with them at all. We should not take anything at face value, we must dig deeper and look at situations from all angles. Our material lives are extremely complex and we do things to one another and then blame God for the outcome, when it is in fact our own actions. Love the people around you and if your family unit breaks up and moves on to another, please make sure that everyone concerned is made to feel loved and secure, especially the children.

Haunting Childhood Memories

A relative of my wife called to see us one evening, as she was worried about a friend of hers who felt that she was being haunted. Each day as she turned off the lights in the evening, something would grab her hand and she would awake each morning to find that her necklace had knots in it. She asked me if there was anything that I could do to help and would I mind going to see her as soon as I could. I seemed to be investigating a lot of haunting at this time; it must have been the time for that pathway of my knowledge to be enhanced. I rang Billy to see if he would come along to support me and as usual he did not let me down.

We got there about eleven o'clock that evening and were greeted by a very frightened lady. She relayed the experiences back to me, just as the relative had said; her neighbour had to come to sit in with her. She told me of the hand that would try to stop her turning off the light and showed me the necklace that was in knots and felt that there was definitely some sort of presence in her home. We sat quietly for a little while with the lights out, as I wanted to see if I could pick up on any vibration in the room. I closed my eyes and went into meditation and as I did this I felt a strong urge to go and put my hands upon the lady's head. I asked her not to be frightened because it was dark in the room.

After a few seconds with my hands on the top of her head a picture came in front of me. I could see a child and she was locked in the attic; there was no furniture in there and no light. The only light that the child could see was through the keyhole. The little girl was dressed in a flimsy nightie and was stood behind the door, peering through the keyhole. She was only a tiny little thing and I could sense that she was shaking with fear. I took my hands from the lady's head and I asked her who was it that used to lock her up. At first she was very quiet and I had to repeat myself. She became hysterical, shouting, 'No, no, no!' 'As a child you were locked up in the attic, there was no light and you stood looking through the keyhole.' She started sobbing and once again cried, 'No, no, no!' I told her that I wanted to bring her back out of that attic, I wanted to bring her back out of that darkness and into the light. The poor woman sat sobbing her heart out and then quietened down and proceeded to tell us the story of when she was child.

She had an older sister and her sister had developed a wart on her throat. It was only a trivial thing, nothing serious, but she went to hospital for it removing. During the simple routine operation something went wrong and her sister died. It affected her mother deeply and she was so afraid of anything happening to her second child that she locked her in the attic. In her state of mind she thought that this was a secure place for the child to be. She did not comprehend how terrifying it was for the poor little girl.

Imagine a child being locked in an attic for two or three hours, all alone and in the dark. The child had grown up and got married and gave birth to six or seven children, all of whom she adored and were her life. Gradually all the children grew up, and in their turn got married and made homes of their own, until eventually only her youngest son was still living with her. The time came for him too to be married and it was at this time that her husband developed terminal cancer. He did not live for very long after the disease developed and suddenly the woman, after caring for her large family for such a long time was all alone. She had no one now and the house was large and empty. There was no one around to comfort her anymore and suddenly she was once again that lonely, frightened, little girl in the attic. Being left alone in the material world is a very strong fear and I believe that in this modern world of ours the lady suffered from what is now termed 'the empty nest syndrome'.

Whatever title we give it loneliness is at its core; we fear being alone. It was made worse for this lady because of her terrible experiences as a child; these fears were at the core of her very being. This had caused the haunting; it was Spirit trying to help her, trying to re-assure her, to let her know that she was not on her own. As she was telling the story, her family, who had come to the house, were gazing around at each other. Not one of them had heard any of this story before. The lady had pushed it away deep into her subconscious; never speaking of it. They knew nothing of what had happened to their mother when she was young, although she had carried it around in her memory for all of those years. Once her last son had gone and her husband had died the old memories of being alone in that dark attic had returned and she was the frightened little girl again.

Spirit had come to console her; to let her know that we are never alone. This lady did not know anything of the spirit world; she did not know that they were there to comfort her. After my visit, her family made arrangements to see her on a regular basis; to surround her with their presence and their love. Now that they were aware of her feelings, they could make sure that someone was with her all of the time. I heard from them some time later and all the strange happenings had stopped. The lady said that she was feeling much happier and more back to her usual self.

It is an awful thing to be alone and those of us who have families must love and cherish them and spend as much time with them as is possible. We are never truly alone, even our families who have passed on into the spirit world are always around us; for love is the tie that binds. We should talk to them, as they are always around and are aware of everything in our lives.

Remember also when you are feeling lonely that there are thousands of others out there, who also need a friend. If you look for them, they will come forward, and you will be of help to each other.

When we think only of ourselves we turn our minds inward

and become pessimistic and lonely. When we think of others, we forget ourselves and suddenly a whole new world, with new people in it opens up. When we forget ourselves and go out there and meet the world halfway lots of good things happen, lots of new people come into our lives. If you are lonely my friend, reach out to others, show an interest in others and the world will come to you. Remember the power of prayer because God is always listening, tell Him of your needs and He will be there to help you.

Arnie the Dog

One of my colleagues in the electrical department at ICI was a chap called George Hayes, he was quite materialistic but nevertheless a very nice man. He never said much as I talked about my healing work, but I knew that he was interested, as he always appeared to be listening. I came home from work one Friday and was gazing out of the window when George's car pulled up. I recognised it straight away, as I saw it daily at work. He looked really upset and came hurriedly up the path. I opened the door before he had a chance to knock and asked what was the matter. 'I need your help Mick, please help me.' He went on to explain that he had to take his dog to the vet that evening, to be put to sleep. His back legs were paralysed and George was heartbroken, he said that he could not bring himself to do it. I told him to go and get his dog and put him down on the path so that I could take a look at him. The poor animal tried to pull his back legs along, but there was no movement in them at all, they were completely paralysed. He had been taking Arnie his dog, to the vets for the last six weeks but was told that nothing could be done.

The vet had advised George that it would be kinder to put him down. I asked him to lift the dog up and carry him over to the Sanctuary. He laid him on the table and I started to give Arnie healing. I did nothing else but lay my hands on him and prayed for him. I then told George to take him home. I told him not to go to the vet that night but to give the dog until Monday. I told him that if he was no better by then he must take him to the vet and do whatever he suggested but he must give him until Monday, no sooner and no later. At that George wrapped his beloved dog in a blanket and carried him to the car. He did not contact me all weekend. I went to work on Monday morning wondering what the response had been and a smiling George greeted me at the gates, he asked me if I would come to his house at lunchtime to see Arnie.

When we arrived Arnie was running around like a puppy.

George told me that he had laid behind his chair for all of Friday night and all day on Saturday, he had not moved at all. George had just sat down to eat his tea, around five o'clock, when Arnie suddenly stood up and walked across the room. He carried on walking around and seemed to be completely better. George had cried with happiness, he had no children and Arnie had been his constant companion, he was his reason for living. Several weeks later George turned up at my house once again with a small package in his hand, he said that it was a birthday gift from Arnie. In it was a wooden plaque with a cross mounted upon it. It was inscribed at the bottom with the words 'Sanctuary of Hope'. I felt very emotional and humbled and kept this plaque in my Sanctuary for many years.

It was brilliant to see his dog back to full health; he lived for about three years after that, but was later knocked down by a car and killed. It is wonderful to know that God's healing powers are not restricted to human beings but to all living creatures. The healing works tremendously well on the animal kingdom, as animals are very receptive and simply accept the love that they are given. They are not inhibited by religious beliefs or pre-conceived ideas. It is a great lesson to learn, God does not only care for people, and God's love is for all, for everyone and everything. We need to remember that life exists in many forms and it is exactly the same life force as we humans have, whether it is in an insect, a plant or an animal. Imagine holding a tiny bird against your chest and feeling its heart beat, its life is just the same as yours. We must have love for all things living and never attempt to kill any form of life.

A Dog Called Benji

Everyone has their own particular story to tell about Mick McGuire and the common thread that runs through them all is their heartfelt gratitude. Whether it is their relative that he has helped or their beloved animals.

I was sitting in his clinic one day when a lady who had heard about the book handed me an envelope. She had written on it 'A Dog Called Benji' and she asked me if I would include her story. This is what it said inside:

In 1993, I was told by the vet, that my much loved little dog, Benji, who was only four years old, would not live for very much longer. He told me that the x-rays that he had taken showed that Benji had an enlarged heart. He was panting all the time, as if he was trying to draw in air and it was getting worse by the day. I was so upset; it felt like the end of my world but I need not have worried. I rang Mick and he told me to bring him straight away for some healing.

We came home that day and my little dog was so much happier, running around and playing. I took him to Mick's regularly for more of the healing and six months later the vet re-examined him and took some more x-rays. To his surprise, Benji's heart had not got any bigger; it was still the same size. I was about to tell the vet that Mick had healed him but I didn't bother. My little dog went on to have a much loved and happy long life. He was about fourteen years old when he finally left me. Mick has cared about my dogs and me for a lot of years now. I owe him more than I could ever say. I pray that God will love and watch over him; he is one on his own and we are very lucky to have him.

Brenda

The Milky Bar Kid

This is a favourite story of Mick's assistant Mavis and one that she loves to tell. She says that the memory of this little lad always makes her smile. We received a call from some people who had recently moved house and had moved from a place called Askern to a house in Doncaster. They said that they felt that the new house was haunted and went on to explain that the wardrobe was being pushed each night in front of the bedroom door. It was a huge, heavy, oak wardrobe and each time it happened their son had to climb out of the window to get out of the room. They heard voices and cries coming from the room and the lights were being switched on and off. She then added that her son was a great one for telling ghost stories and that all the kids at school were afraid of him. She said that he frightened his brothers and sisters with his tales and she felt sure that he had something to do with it all.

We agreed to go and visit the new house to see if we could help and were introduced to all of the family. The way that she had described her son, we expected to see a great big lad but there in front of us was a tiny, little thing. He was wearing little round glasses, which is why Mavis nicknamed him 'The Milky Bar Kid'. This child could never have moved such a huge wardrobe.

His ghost stories must have been well told, as he certainly could not frighten anybody. I asked him not to be afraid but to come and sit on the stool next to me. I gently put my hands upon his head to see what the vibrations were. I did feel the vibrations of something quite sinister but it was not the little one. I told him to sit down and asked his mum if she would mind sitting on the stool. Immediately as I touched her I felt the heat. I had a picture of huge flames licking up to the ceiling and children screaming with their nightgowns on fire. Mavis was sat at the other side of the room and she too could see the flames and hear the children screaming.

Then the boy's uncle came through, who was killed in a

motorbike accident. He pointed at the lad and shouted 'Be a good boy.' All of this was nothing at all to do with the boy but was most definitely linked to the mother. The lady was a psychic but she did not know it. There had been a fire at some time in the other house where she lived in Askern and all the children who lived there were burnt to death. The children, who had passed in the fire, had linked with her and were moving the wardrobes to let her know that they were around.

Unfortunately it was not her bedroom but the young boy's. I explained all of this to her and she looked at me in complete shock. She asked me if I could help her to develop her psychic skills but I was so busy at that time that I had to refuse. I was then the head of the Spiritualist Church in Doncaster and was training the now famous Rosemary Altea but I advised the woman as to where to go for more development. The thing that still makes us smile about it all is the look on the little lad's face, as while we were investigating, he had a cushion pinned firmly over his face and kept peeping back over the top and ducking back down again. He had been playing with these children in his room and they were real children to him.

I wonder if he still scares the kids at school with his ghost stories?

Dark Depths of Suicide: Low Vibrations

This story is about a lady who called on me about another haunting. She had been really poorly for quite a while and had huge, dark circles under her eyes. I remember psychically thinking that there was something seriously wrong with her. From the information that this lady gave me, I felt that this was going to be a bad experience.

She went on to explain that, when she was watching the television at home, the wires would come out and start to fly around in mid-air and a black cloud hovered over the room.

I knew that if this was correct, then this was a particularly bad haunting.

I asked her to tell me all about herself and she told me that she had suffered a nervous breakdown. I asked her if she had tried to take her own life and she confided that yes, she had. I went to her house to look into the matter; it seemed to be a part of my development at that time to help with places that were haunted. I tuned into the vibrations; this poor lady had obviously been very low. She had made her vibrations so low that she had drawn a spirit entity to her and at the point when she had tried to commit suicide one of the spirits from the lower realms had attached itself to her.

Her neighbour went on to tell me that she had been present in the house when the television went haywire and the black cloud appeared. She said the Lord's Prayer to help them both. I took the large black cross with me that I kept on the wall of my Sanctuary. I don't know the reason why I did this, other than I felt that it was a little bit of support from the Sanctuary, which was a place of prayers and healing. The more the vibrations came, the more I realised that this woman was in a lot of trouble. The Spirit was trying to get her to commit suicide again, it wanted control of her spirit, and it wanted her for itself.

My only option was to allow this entity to come through me so I tried to fully explain to the woman what I was doing and hoped that she would understand the severity of her situation. She started to tell me about the noises that she heard coming from the attic and had not spoken of these before. The noises had made her so afraid of going up there, that she had nailed the attic door shut. I asked her if she possessed a pair of pliers that I could go and take the nails out with. I took my dog Sally with me, as animals are very perceptive; they sense Spirit before human beings do. I grabbed my torch and shouted for Sally to follow me but she just sat there and would not move.

It was really dark up there, as no lights had been installed; I shone the torch and removed all the nails from the door. I climbed up and started to have a look around but my torch went out and everything was pitch black. I shook the torch but I knew that the batteries were new ones. I remember thinking that I must keep a steady nerve; this entity was a bad one. I started to whistle to console myself and carefully walked all around the walls looking all around me and then I made my way back to the door. I could not get out of there fast enough. I was very glad to be down that ladder.

The presence in this house was a very serious force to contend with and I sat down and went into a deep meditation. I decided to go into trance and allow the Spirit to come through me. This was not a thing that anyone should do; it is an extremely dangerous practice. I knew that I was well protected, my spirit guides are of the highest order and will not let me down and I have absolute faith in them.

This voice came through, 'You are mine, and you belong to me.' The woman sat watching and shouted 'I do not, I do not!' 'You belong to me, you gave up your life and now it is mine.' There began a shouting match between them with a great deal of nastiness. The entity screamed at her,

'You will take your life and you will give it to me.' It kept repeating and repeating that she belonged to him. He kept on saying that she did not want her life and now it was his and told her time and time again to take her life, as it was his now to do as he wished with. The screaming match continued and she screamed back at him, 'I will not do this!'

A look of comprehension suddenly came over her face and I could see that she realised now that by trying to commit suicide she had left herself wide open for another spirit to take over her spirit; she had entered into the realms of darkness where he had latched on to her. The arguing lasted for quite a while and they both screamed at each other and then I intervened. I came back to my body and asked him to leave. He said that he would take me, but he had no chance; I was much stronger than that. The poor woman looked in a state of shock. There was no wonder that her soul was tormented, that her eyes were black and she was so ill.

I asked her how she felt now and she told me that she was very frightened and would never try to commit suicide again; she would never allow that man to own her. I told her to keep my cross for protection. I had it for many years and it had been through a lot of healings; I knew that her need was great. I had done my job here now; I had secured the safety of her soul.

It is important to know that there are bad spirits around as well as good ones. There are spirits around just waiting for a weakness; for someone who allows their spirit to sink to the depths. We can be unaware that they latch themselves on to us. For young people playing around with ouija boards, not knowing really what they are dealing with, it is extremely dangerous.

It is very important when dealing with spiritual matters that we are aware that we are dealing with a real world.

We would not want our children to wander into somewhere that was strange; somewhere where there may be wicked people waiting to pick them up. It is the same with the spirit world, there are good and bad souls the same as here. There are laws; laws that govern our spirits and one of those is that we do not take our own life. We can become trapped between the two worlds where all sorts of bad things can happen. In this material life, face everything as you meet it; deal with it if you can and if you cannot then let it go and move on. Safeguard your spirit all of the time and do not let things get you down.

The health of the lady improved after I visited her and I rang her on several occasions to check that she was still okay. This lesson is to tell us how when things affect us here on the material plane then that in turn affects the spirit world for it is not a separate part of our daily lives but an integrated part. We are eternally spirit and we must try to ensure that our spirit progresses throughout life. We must take the responsibility for adding positively to our own lives and to that of our fellow man.

I placed a blessing upon the woman but also a blessing upon the entity. I hoped that it would learn a better path and would move on to better things.

Lost Faith

Mary came to my clinic suffering with a back and neck problem, she had some manipulation and the machines on her back and finally went upstairs for a massage with Doreen, my assistant. During the massage Mary told Doreen that she had spent a lot of money going to see different mediums and some of them were quite famous but continued to say that she had lost all her faith, as not one of them had given her the information that she was looking for.

When people come to my clinic, they often come for physiotherapy or one of the alternative treatments. They are unaware of the healing and psychic work that I do and unless people ask me I do not tell them about it.

Doreen explained to Mary that I was a psychic and a healer but told her that I do not do readings anymore, as the healing work is now my priority. When she came downstairs she begged me to do a reading for her and I did have a little time spare that day, so I told her that I would give her some healing to see if anything came through.

On laying my hands upon Mary I saw a young man in America; he was gay and a drug addict and he had recently moved into a house that Mary owned. I sent up prayers for help and Mary's mother came. She told me that it was not easy but she was trying to help the lad, as he was Mary's son. Mary's face lit up like a beacon when I told her, 'That is fantastic, that is what I wanted to hear.' She went on to tell me her story:

'I divorced my first husband, who was a police officer and my son has now come home from America and he is living in our former home. He is always dressed in a white gown with a white turban and walks around in a drug-induced state.' The question that was eating away at her was that he might take an overdose. I told her that he was certainly in danger of doing this but a lot of people were praying for him in the hope that he can be saved. I told her to go home and to pray for him each day. She was so overcome with emotion that my assistant had to help her. She said that she could not believe that a stranger had given her all this information and one week later her husband rang and asked if he too could have the healing and a reading. I told him that I did not do readings anymore.

Her son did actually overdose but fortunately help came quickly and he made an excellent recovery.

The Were-Wolf

Lunchtime at the clinic is always a relaxed affair; we work so hard but for an hour each day we chat and let the cares of the day pass by. We have a cosy little English kitchen filled with coffee mugs, easy chairs and easy chatter. We sit and recollect things that have gone on during our working lives; some wonderful, some miraculous, and some tragic. One particular story that is often mentioned is the one that we nicknamed 'The Were-Wolf. It sounds like something out of a horror movie and is so bizarre that it sounds unbelievable but it is perfectly true.

This man made an appointment to see me at the Sanctuary at my home and we had a normal telephone conversation about a back injury and nothing seemed at all unusual. I have never been a person to judge anyone by appearance but when this man visited me the way that he looked made me shudder; his whole apparel was sinister. He looked like a sort of Al Capone character but darker; he was dressed in a full-length black coat and wore a trilby hat. His body language was very closed, his hands dug deep into his pockets and his shoulders were hunched downwards. His eyes were narrow and flitting nervously all around the room and his vibration was distinctly negative. I welcomed him into the healing room and my assistant asked to take his coat. He suddenly noticed the cross on the back wall and he took several steps backwards, staggering about like a drunken man. I beckoned him towards the couch but he walked backwards, avoiding eye contact with my cross. I looked over to Mavis and her face told me that she was thinking exactly the same as I was.

At that time I had a Labrador dog called Sally, she was quite an old lady and unsteady on her legs. Normally, she would sit all day long, quietly under the two wooden benches in the Sanctuary, while I did my work. She was shuffling around and seemed restless, I am always aware of the movements of animals, as they are very receptive.

The man took off his coat to reveal a black shirt, black tie and black trousers; he was quite a thin, wiry man. As he lay down on the couch, I felt uneasy and I exchanged several concerned glances with Mavis. Speech is not always necessary, the eyes are very proficient communicators and our eye contact said it all. After manipulating his back for about fifteen minutes we commenced with the laying on of hands. I felt a huge tremor, like a volcano just before it erupts. Mavis's eyes were popping out of her head and I knew that she was experiencing the same as me. I half-smiled and nodded in reassurance to her. We have worked together for so long that there is an affinity between us and I knew that Mavis trusted me to keep her safe.

His body slowly rose, getting higher and higher so we pressed down hard and carried on with the healing. As his body lowered down on to the couch again, a revolting, gurgling sound came from him and he began retching and belching in a pronounced and disgusting manner.

Then his mouth opened, as wide as his jaws would allow and out of it, between the rotting, yellow teeth, came a tongue, it was long and horrible. He snarled and growled and lashed out with his tongue towards Mavis, baring those awful, long teeth. She jumped back startled with a look of total disbelief on her face and my gaze remained steadfastly upon hers. I pressed my hands down upon his body and I pressed so hard that my shoulders ached. Mavis seemed to compose herself a little and then did the same. Sally the dog bolted out of the door at breakneck speed; I have never seen those old legs move so fast. The man retched again and again and the smell of sour vomit came from his mouth and he was still trying to reach Mavis with his tongue.

Some twenty minutes passed, his body was falling and rising, he was retching and snarling until finally he settled, his contorted features resumed their normal place again.

He looked really embarrassed and asked in a sarcastic tone, 'What was all that about.' I closed my eyes and took a moment to get my breath back; it had been hard work. I went over to the bowl to wash my hands; I was angry, extremely angry. Turning on him I shouted, 'You know very well what all that was about and so do I, you have been going alone into the attic where you live and have been practising levitation and using a ouija board. A lower entity has entered your body and I have just released you from it.'

The smirk dropped from his face and I started on him again. 'This Sanctuary is only for the good, all that I do is for the good and I never, ever want to see you here again.' He dressed quickly and left and I telephoned his mother to make sure that he was okay and she said that he was. Thankfully I have never seen him since that day.

The only light-hearted thing that I can say about this story and I chuckle to myself every time I think of them, is of the two men who were waiting in the corridor. They were two hefty labourers from a town called Barnsley, which is an extremely tough mining area of Yorkshire. On hearing the horrendous noise and then Sally the dog shooting past them, they thought that this was all part of the treatment and consequently that they would be put through the same. They promptly decided that their backs were not too bad after all and maybe they would go home and take a couple of paracetemol. They too have never been seen again.

A Traumatized Mind in a Frozen World

A further miracle that happened to me was the healing of my wife's aunt. She was not really an aunt, not a blood relative, but an old family friend a neighbour who had always helped them over the years. About thirty years before I saw her, when she was much younger, she had lost a baby and this affected her deeply. The consequences were that it traumatized her mind. From the day that she lost the child she had not spoken to anyone again; she could not wash, feed or take care of herself and was totally reliant on the people around her. Her family rang my wife to see if there was any way that I could help, so she told them to come along and said that I would take a look at her. When they arrived my wife put on a bit of a tea for them.

I took aunty and her husband into my sanctuary and started as always with the physiotherapy; stretching her neck and joints and putting the massage machine on to her back. I gave it a good massage to get all the circulation going. I made her comfortable for the healing; the lights were soft and I said a prayer and began the laying on of hands. I turned on the lights and went to ask her how she felt but I did not expect her to answer me because she had not uttered a word for many years. She said 'Michael that was absolutely beautiful.' I know that this always happens after the healing but each time is still as wondrous as the first, I still get wrapped up in the emotion of it all.

I took her and her husband back into the dining room, where everyone was just about to have tea. All the family were there and my wife came over to aunty with a cup of tea already in her hand. She leaned forward and asked if aunty would like a sandwich, never expecting a reply. 'Ooh yes please Dorothy, I would love some, I am really hungry,' and at that she walked over to the table and helped herself to the sandwiches and cakes. Her husband stood staring at her and he started to cry. She came back and asked him if he was all right. 'Yes dear,' he replied, 'I am fine, are you?'

All the family were silent, just standing there watching the scene; it was as if she had woken up from a long dream, or maybe even a nightmare. It seemed that since she lost the baby that her world had been frozen in time and she could not move on. The healing had brought her back to the real world instead of the one inside herself. She never came back to me again; she did not have to, as she was so much better. She was back to washing and cooking and cleaning; back to the woman that she had been before her loss. Somehow the healing had reached her particular need; it healed that horrible gap that had formed in her at her bereavement. The healing was instantaneous. God and Spirit can do things that we cannot even begin to contemplate. There are no limits be the need physical or mental; God can cure anything.

Distance, Space & Time:
Family Stories

I am often asked where my psychic ability comes from, did my parents have this gift or my grandparents and did they also have the gift of healing?

As in most families, stories have been handed down from generation to generation and whether they have been changed in the telling I do not know, but I will endeavour to tell them to you, as they were told to me. I would like to tell you a story that my grandmother told me about during the war, because I believe that she too had psychic abilities.

Her son, my uncle Bill, was at war, fighting the Japanese. One day the Ministry of Defence sent her a letter that everyone dreaded receiving at that time, which was to say that he was missing, presumed dead. I cannot imagine how she felt, being told that her son was dead; it would have caused her the most terrible distress. I will tell you her story as she told it to me.

She went to bed one night, after hearing the news of her son and she prayed. She asked God if he could give her a message to let her know if her son really was dead, because she felt in her heart that he was alive. Had he passed or was he still here somewhere? She desperately needed to know. Missing in action is never enough; it always leaves room for a mother's hope that her son will one day walk through her door again.

As she fell into a deep sleep, she found herself walking through a dense jungle then she came to a clearing, which was the entrance to a hospital. There was a large board with a name across the top of it and it was an open-air hospital. She went inside and walked along the left hand side to either the seventh or the eighth bed and there in the bed was Bill, her son. He was covered in scabs of some sort and she went to hug him and he said, 'I am all right Mother, I am alive.' She awoke from the dream sobbing but feeling so much better.

She came down to tell all the family that Bill was alive. He was in a Japanese hospital and was thin and covered in scabs but he was alive. Everyone tried to comfort her, believing that she was in denial of her son's death but each time anyone spoke of his death she stated adamantly that he was still alive. It was several months later when she received the letter to say that Bill had been found and he was in fact a Japanese prisoner of war, none of the family could believe it.

The day that he returned home finally came, which was of course an occasion of much celebration and it was then that he confirmed her story. He told her of the name on the board over the hospital and that he was in the seventh bed on the left hand side. It was quite incredible that she had given all of this information to the family and it was most certainly a psychic experience. She did call it a dream at the time but now, knowing so much of psychic experiences, I know that she travelled back in time; back to the jungle where her son was lying in a sick bed.

Distance, space and time mean nothing in the spirit world and a mother's love will most certainly exceed all of that and she was able to travel there to see him. It is a strange thing but when people die the customary knocks are always heard, sometimes two knocks and sometimes three. It may be on a door or on the wall but it does not matter where you are, you can be on a cruise liner upon the ocean, if one of your loved ones passes over, Spirit will know exactly where to come to let you know.

If only each one of us were taught the truth from birth about our connection to all things; to the Universe, to the spirit world from whence we came and to God. We would not then switch off the senses that link our very being to all things. Instead of strife and unhappiness, we would know love and joy, peace and wholeness. Never forget my friend that you are Spirit, you are part of all that is and part of you is of God.

Lessons From The World of Spirit

As with everything in life, the more that we think that we know, the more that we find there is to learn. Life is a continuum of learning and it never ceases. The learning may be in relationships, careers, personal development, any arena but it is continuous throughout our lives. My lessons from the world of Spirit have been innumerable, so much to learn and so little time, as they say. Spirit always waited for me to enter into sleep state to then take me on journeys to obtain knowledge. They showed me where people who have done evil are and what was happening to them. They showed me people who had been killed during the wars and how to rescue them; to see them safely forward into the Spirit world.

I found myself rescuing people, who had been in firing squads. I would go and stand beside them and we would all be shot. We would all fall down and I would tell everyone to stand up; that we were okay, that everything was all right now. I would then escort them safely away to the Spirit world. A lot of people linger on around the Earth plane because they do not know what has happened to them or where they should go. Spirit made me face all of my fears; I would see these as terrifying dreams but they were actually very important lessons. I had to learn about caring for people, not only from our world but from the Spirit world as well. Spirit would gesture for me to come forward and would place me where I would look at things to overcome my fears. They needed to give me a good grounding and philosophy on life, so that I was able to heal every sort of condition. Where the journeys would lead me, I never knew; I simply trusted my guides and followed. It is fantastic to know that life has a purpose and that we come to this Earth plane to learn, to understand and to come to terms with everything. The Earth plane is our school.

Here we have illnesses, pain and suffering. We can lose the people that we love, our parents, grandparents, and friends, even our precious children. We suffer terribly mentally and emotionally as well as physically; life as we know can be extremely cruel.

This is why there is such a great need for LOVE; to love and support each other in every way possible, making all of our pathways easier. Nothing in this material plane that we live on is more precious a gift than love for without it we cannot survive.

At the end of our lives here on Earth we are finally free; our soul becomes free, free of the restrictions of the physical body, free of all the pain and suffering. We once again meet all the loved ones that we have lost; the ones who have gone on to Spirit before us. They are always beside us here on Earth but we actually get to meet them once again; to be given their love once again when we go back home. Our life here on Earth is so short that we must every day appreciate the people around us, indeed everything that is around us; all of our blessings. Never let a day pass by without telling your people that you love them and cherishing everything that is good in your life.

We have to face everything that confronts us on a daily basis. We need to ask God for courage and strength to overcome all of our obstacles and to always support each other. We must always look forward and never back. All that we need to take from the past are the lessons that it has taught us, so that we do not repeat them again and again. Learn as much in your lifetime as you possibly can so that when it is your time you can take back to the spirit world a loving, courageous and knowledgeable spirit.

Clairaudience: Saved by Spirit

This story is about the time that Spirit saved the lives of my family and me. It was a lovely mid-summer's day and we had spent it visiting my wife's sister and about eleven o'clock in the evening we set off for home. We were all very relaxed and chatting about the events of the day. The country roads were very quiet but suddenly, out of the blue, I received a message from Spirit. I was told that we were all going to be killed in a road accident; I couldn't believe what I was hearing. The thought of the death of my whole family was unthinkable and I began to panic, changing gear and slowing down. The children asked me what was wrong and I didn't answer then my wife asked me again. I did not tell my wife the full truth but told her that there was going to be an accident with our car. She said that maybe we should turn back but as I pointed out to her, the accident could still happen going the other way. A blind panic came over me and I started to drive erratically. My wife who was sitting beside me, said calmly, 'Ask Spirit what to do.' Why hadn't I thought of that? In my confusion, this blatantly obvious solution had not occurred to me.

I asked Spirit who instructed me to slow down, so I dropped my speed to less than 25mph, crawling along and praying at the same time. Every time a vehicle came into view, I found myself tensing, was this the end? We had travelled about eight miles down the road, when the scene of an accident appeared. The car had its bonnet embedded into a tree and there was shattered glass all over the road. Smoke was coming from the engine. It must have happened only minutes earlier as there was a frenzy of activity. The driver was being assisted and other motorists were braking hard to stop and offer help. One of the other drivers informed me that he had telephoned the emergency services. It seemed that the car came over the hill at high speed, lost control and spun over to the other side of the road, it turned upside down and was finally halted by the tree. I know that had I continued at my normal speed that we would most certainly have been involved in that accident. I said a prayer of thanks as the voice of Spirit had saved our lives and I also prayed for the people in the accident.

It was at this point in my life that my psychic was becoming stronger; I was given the gift of clairaudience or hearing spirit voices. I remember one night, just as I was going to sleep, I heard the most beautiful singing; it was the voice of Gracie Fields. I woke up and told my wife that Gracie was about to pass over. She was not really listening, so I told her again. 'Gracie Fields is going to pass in the next few days.' During the week my wife never mentioned it again, I think that she was growing so used to me saying unusual things to her. My friend Billy called as usual on the Thursday evening to go to the healing night at the church and mentioned during the conversation that Gracie Fields had passed away in her home. My wife looked at me in the way that wives do and remembered me telling her on the previous Sunday that this would happen.

I feel very honoured to be a spiritual medium. It has not been a quick thing for me but has taken a long, long time to develop; all that I have done is to carry on and to heed the word of my tutors. If you are considering developing your psychic awareness, then find yourself an excellent tutor. It is much the same as anything else; we need to start at the very beginning and our guides will gradually increase our knowledge as they see fit but remember that the spirit world is as real as our world, so please make sure that you work only for God and for the good of others.

The Psychiatric Patient

Some of the stories that I have to tell are very frightening; I have had a number of alarming experiences while doing my psychic work. One that springs to mind is the story of a young woman in a wheelchair, who was only about eighteen or nineteen years old. I treated her in the bungalow, where she lived with her grandmother. She came in to my clinic one day with a beaming smile across her face and looked really happy for once. She said that she would like me to meet her new boyfriend. I think that for some reason she wanted my approval, which was very nice. I told her that I would come to see her in a few days' time and that I would look forward to meeting him.

I went to the bungalow a few days later as promised during the evening after work. The young girl was there in the wheelchair and her boyfriend was standing beside her. He was a tall, slim looking lad and she introduced us. I stepped forward to shake his hand and as I did so she said, 'He suffers with his stomach Mick.' As my hand reached closer to him and I went into his aura, I knew that this man suffered with more than his stomach. He never actually touched me; he moved quickly away and sharply rushed out of the door, slamming it violently as he went out. I needed to tell this girl of the terrible danger that she was in; I knew that this man was a killer and his intentions were to kill her and her grandmother, I was absolutely certain of that.

My interpretation of this person was not wrong; the vibrations that I picked up from him were dark and sinister. I tried to explain this to her and advised her never to see him again. What I was telling her was the truth but she started to cry and shouted for him to come back. Thankfully he had already gone.

I begged her to please listen to what I was saying to her, to please take this seriously. I was not trying to scare monger but merely warn her of the facts. 'This man will kill you and he will kill your grandmother.' I had to put the message across over and over again. I told her that the feeling that I got from him was so fierce, so overpowering. She was by this time sobbing and took quite a lot of calming down and I personally felt shaken and afraid and was glad to be out of there.

Here was an extremely dangerous, severely mentally ill man, walking the streets and he was capable of killing at any time. He was very good looking and looked like your average guy, which is why the poor girl had fallen for him. I told my wife that she must not open the door to anyone and that she must ring me immediately, if a stranger came to the door, because I knew that something dreadful was imminent. What I felt from him was really bad; I knew that he could kill without thought or remorse and I had never dealt with this level of malevolence before.

My wife rang me later to say that something had happened at the girl's bungalow and would I go there immediately, as the police were already there. Several police cars were parked outside and some members of her family had arrived. The young girl in the wheelchair looked distraught and told me that she had been hit in the face. I felt relieved to see that she was alive.

The brother of this man was at the house, although I didn't know why and I went over to speak to him. I asked him if he could tell me how his brother had killed his grandfather. His chin fell to the floor, when I said this; I could see that he was trying to work out how I knew this information. He started to tell me what had happened. Not only had his brother killed him; he had chopped his grandfather into pieces and the room was awash with his blood. His fixation now was that he was going to chop his mother's head off. The police were called and managed to restrain him.

I had known instinctively that the feelings that I picked up from him were correct. I know that out in our world there are people, who are affected with this evilness, there are people who murder, people who prey on young women or children. They have the same inner thoughts as this man and are capable of killing at random with no thought or conscience. They will mutilate and torture; these people have an intrinsically evil spirit.

It is a very frightening thing to think of and we must be aware that people like this exist; we must be aware in order to protect ourselves and our families.

The girl rang me the next day and asked if I would go to visit him in the hospital. I told her that I would go on the Wednesday afternoon, although I was not happy about it. It was not a pleasant place to go. He was lying on the bed and as I walked towards him he sat bolt upright, he was attempting to make his body higher than mine; to look down on me. I knew his game; he was putting himself in what he thought was a position of power.

'Do not do that to me, young man because it won't work,' I told him, never taking my eyes away from his. I have seen this sort of intimidation too many times before. He lowered his eyes, he was no match for me and he knew it. He turned to his girlfriend and said 'Should I tell Mick?' 'Yes,' came the barely audible reply.

He was from a secure psychiatric hospital called Rampton. It is a hospital for the criminally insane and he was there on a life licence. I asked him what he had done and he said that he had killed his grandfather. He told me that his grandfather had hit him and he had a knife so he stabbed the old man and killed him. I couldn't shake off these abhorrent feelings I had about him; this man was an extremely deranged and dangerous person.

He told me that for a while now something had been following him, something that was spinning very fast. When he went to use the telephone, it was there in the doorway blocking the entrance and it would knock the receiver off when he went to use the telephone. He told me that it was also on the desk in the psychiatrist's office. 'I am not telling him that though, because if I do I will never get out of here. I need you to help me.' He was still using the 'I am in charge' tone.

I was a little unsure of how to face what I was feeling, as I couldn't shake off this awful feeling of dread. This is a feeling that is normally quite alien to me, as I am so protected by my wonderful spirit guides but the intrinsic evil of this man made me fearful. It is horrible to think that this level of malevolence exists but it does. I prayed for this man that God may bless him and that he may see the light.

It was a frightening experience for me as a psychic, as sometimes during our work as psychics, we can place ourselves in positions of danger. Men come to women psychics for private readings, when they are at home alone. This should always be discouraged and I try to tell psychics to keep a sensible attitude and do not invite people into your home that you do not know unless someone else is present. Many psychics only book women and this is a safe thing to do sometimes, to maybe only book men when another man is around.

In the spirit world, as in our world, both good and evil exist. We talk about the God side, but there is also the darker side, always that fear. I am always very thankful that I have very good spiritual helpers. My doorkeeper, the person that looks after me, is Red Feather and he will only allow people through who are right and good. He is not just my guide; he is a universal guide, an omnipotent protector, very powerful and very strong. He is always there during my spiritual development and I thank God for him every day; he is such a wise and wonderful person and spirituality so strong and safe. I know that he will always take care of me and I ask you to take care of yourselves and your loved ones at all times. Be vigilant. Do not allow negative people into your lives and always be aware of your feelings. If your intuition tells you that something is wrong, then act upon it. Safeguard your families and never trust someone simply because they look okay, go always with how you feel.

Psychosomatic:
Our Imaginary World

A young girl had been off school for a number of weeks suffering from stomach pains and had been to see her doctor and then to the hospital, all of whom could find no reason for the pain, so her grandparents brought her to the clinic to see if I could help.

I talked to her for a little while and counselled her; she told me that her parents had split up and were about to be divorced. The pain and hurt of the split showed in her face, I knew that her problem was of an emotional nature. I explained to her that she was not losing either her mother or her father and that they both still loved her very much but they did not want to live with each other any more. I asked her if she could try her best to be grown up in what she was thinking and to try to help the split between her parents be as easy as possible. I told her to be strong and to not be afraid; to keep her faith, as God would guide and help her. She was being made to make decisions like a grown up when she was only a child but I did my best to reassure her that everything would turn out all right and that both her mother and her father would always see her. I gave the child some healing, which made her calmer and more at peace with herself.

I never heard anything of her again until about two years later, when a couple came into the clinic. They said that I had been recommended by an elderly couple, whose granddaughter I had treated a few years ago. I was pleased to hear of the young girl again and asked how she was and they told me that she returned to school the day after I treated her and that all her pain had disappeared. So often our pains are psychosomatic. As you may know dear reader, the word comes from the joining of two words, psyche, meaning the mind and soma, meaning the body. The two are powerful allies and work in conjunction with each other; when one is upset, the other cannot fail to be upset also. Pain and fear exists within the mind long before it manifests itself within the body. Healing is very powerful in curing psychosomatic illness, as well as physical ailments.

So is the power of prayer. If we could all say a simple prayer each night, maybe to help us through the difficulties of that day it would help so much. If all is right in your world dear friend, then pray for someone else; send out a loving thought to someone, who has a problem or ask for healing for someone who is sick.

I remember one day, while driving to work, my mind felt heavy with all the problems that were going on in my life. I was listening to the radio and there was a programme being broadcast, around nine a.m., which was done by the Reverend Roger Royle and it was called, Pause For Thought. It was to pause for a moments thought each day and each day the Reverend gave out a different lesson. Today's lesson was, 'Are you seeing things as they really are?' He asked about all the situations that face us daily. Do we see them with real clarity? Do we see them as they really are or as we think they are? How often is our perception of reality distorted?

This lesson set me thinking; was I not looking at my own problems properly, was I being blinkered in the way that I looked at them? Perhaps they were not as bad as I perceived them to be. I offered a prayer up to God, as I sat at the wheel of my car, Dear God, please let me see things as they really are not as I think they are. Nothing happened, but I suddenly felt cheerier and more contented within myself; all the heaviness seemed lifted from me. I realised that I did not have any real problems; my world was quite wonderful really.

All the problems were in my mind; I had created the down feeling myself. We make our own minds confused by filling them with trivial things; things that we convince ourselves are momentous. We should all pray every day and every night; we should ask for clarity, ask God that we may see things more clearly. Maybe then we would not hurt somebody that we do not need to; maybe it would even stop a murder. We need to realise that other people are lost in this world; that other people need our help. We all get mixed up in our thoughts, which in turn mix up our actions. The sages of many years before us would meditate for clarity of thought, as it is so important to see things from all angles; to see the bigger picture.

We need to be aware of all the blessings that surround us; the blessings that are from God; from a sunny day to the good food on your plate. If we follow God, we would not kill; not even the tiniest creature and the world would be a far, far, better place. Please ask for God's help in all that you think and all that you do.

This is an imaginary world and nothing is more important than our thoughts, for our thoughts create the reality in which we live. A building is not constructed without it first being an idea in someone's mind and a plan of any sort is created in the mind, before it ever takes place in reality. Be careful what you think my friend; make your thoughts positive and good and plan everything that you think and do cautiously and with love. The Earth plane can be your heaven or it can be your hell; for it to be your heaven then you first have to walk with God. Say a prayer dear friend this evening and ask for your thoughts to be clear and your thoughts and deeds to be positive. Let us all aim for a better world to live in.

A Dream Come True

Sue and Patrick were two people who came to my clinic for healing to help with their IVF treatment. When Sue heard that a book was being written about my work, she said that she would like to add her own story.

This is the letter that she sent to me:

12th February 2002

Our story starts back in November 1999, when my father was a patient of Mick McGuire's. One day as my mother sat in the waiting room while my father had his treatment, she noticed some cards on the coffee table. One of them was for a lady who did spiritual readings and her name was June. My mother immediately thought about me, as I was desperate for some answers in my life. I wanted to know if my IVF treatment would work next year.

We have been trying for a baby now for well over eight years; we tried all sorts of different treatments but in the end had to resort to IVF. The first two attempts were unsuccessful and we had already spent fifteen thousand pounds trying for a baby but we were desperate; our lives were just not complete. We wanted a baby so badly and I became very stressed, as we were putting all our hopes on the third attempt. This was in February 2000.

Going back to November 1999, I made an appointment to see June, who was a lovely lady and picked up on all the problems that I had and told me that I would have a baby girl the following year. June also told me how Mick has helped other ladies like me, who have problems conceiving; how he has used the healing to help them to conceive. She told me how lots of them went to him with little hope of ever having a child and advised me to go to see him. I made an appointment over the phone and told Mick all of our problems. He sounded very nice and seemed like a person that you could talk to easily and said that he would do his best to help us.

The following week I went for my first healing. I felt very stressed and a bit nervous and Mick picked up on this but he and Mavis his assistant soon made me feel reassured and relaxed. Mick told me stories about other ladies, who had the same problem and now have children of their own. At first I thought to myself, how is it possible for him to do this? Now that I know how great Mick is at healing, it is like a documentary that you see on television; you don't believe it until you see it happen. What Mick does is unbelievable.

I enjoyed every minute of my first session of healing; there was soothing music playing and the healing was wonderful. Mick started at my head and went all the way down my body to my feet; he then pulled and moved my feet about to remove the stress in my body. About half an hour after my healing sessions I got pain around my ovaries; not really bad pain but sharp period type pains. To me this felt as if that part of my body was coming back to life again, it was working again. This always happened straight after the healing.

By the time February 2000 arrived, I felt really positive about my next IVF treatment. I relaxed and remembered what Mick and June had told me and somehow I knew in my mind that this time I was going to have a baby, I knew that the healing that I had been given would work. Mick and Mavis wished me luck and I went for my next treatment in mid-February 2000. The most stressful part of IVF treatment is that you have to wait two weeks for the results and the waiting to see if anything has happened is awful. I felt different about it this time though, more positive.

It was good news; after trying for eight years I was finally pregnant and we were over the moon. I could not wait to tell Mick our news; I knew that it was thanks to his help that I was finally having a baby. Without Mick's healing I don't think that we would have ever had a child of our own. He is the one person who helped us the most and for that we are so very grateful.

I gave birth to a beautiful baby girl, Charlotte, on 1st November 2000 and when we look at her we still cannot believe that we *have got her here today. Charlotte is our dream and has made our life complete. We have decided that we would like to try for a brother or sister for Charlotte and I have already made my appointment with Mick, before I go back on the IVF again. I would not even attempt it without the help of his wonderful healing. The Healerman is unbelievable and is now a dear friend of ours, as are all the girls in the clinic.*

Thank you all so much,

Love

Sue, Patrick and Charlotte

Classes of Learning:

Life Skills & Zero Tolerance

A skill that has always intrigued me is the art of hypnosis, I have watched hypnotists work on the television and on stage over the years and find it fascinating how powerful the mind is and how people can be controlled by it. Because of all the psychic work that I do, I have often sat and thought that it was perhaps self-hypnosis. I had my first experience of picking up on the conditions of other people in the church, when I felt that I had an injection of cocaine and found that it was actually someone who had been to the dentist that day. I did not know at the time that I was a sensitive; that I would need to ask for these conditions to be removed, as they were not actually mine. In those early days I often thought that I had hypnotised myself.

The subject interested me so much that I decided that I would study it properly; I would look for somewhere that did courses on hypnotherapy. I enrolled at the Northern School of Hypnosis. The group met in a small place called Howden and we were introduced to the tutors who were Peter, Val and Angela. They were very approachable, likeable people, who made us all feel comfortable and welcome. The course was fascinating. I had sat in many meditation classes and was taught that particular art thoroughly but this was a completely new area of work for me. We were given books to teach us the theory of hypnosis and then practise during the afternoon.

Peter used to say that he did not have any visualisation skills but yet he taught us the skill wonderfully. I found all of the lessons really pleasurable and I also remember that Peter was having problems with his neck and I examined it for him one morning. I manipulated it a little and gave him some healing and he said that he was amazed that the pain had disappeared and that he felt so much better he had almost the full rotation of his neck back.

They were a very mixed bunch on the course; Peter told me that he would often get people who were tarot card readers, psychics or counsellors. People who were interested in all avenues of alternative medicine, covering a wide range of different treatments. We attended the hypnosis seminars every weekend for around six months. I was totally captivated by the work that we did and knew that I would certainly put all the knowledge that I had gained into practice. I now have my Masters Certificate in Hypnotherapy and its uses have been immeasurable. I have used my hypnotherapy skills not only to help my clients but it has also proved to be a great asset in my own life.

It became really important when my wife developed cancer, as I gave Dorothy several sessions of hypnosis during the treatment of her illness. I hypnotised her for the chemotherapy; for having injections and blood tests and for going through the M.R.I. scan. My wife was phobic about confined spaces, so she was dreading the scan and was terrified of needles. I was able to use hypnosis to help her get through the hospital visits and the traumatic cancer treatments. I combined the healing with the hypnosis and this proved to be really powerful, making her feel calm and in control. It actually helped both of us to get through several months of her treatment.

My special thanks go out to the people who taught me this skill, Peter, Val and Angela and I thank them for their effortless work in teaching people to use hypnosis correctly and ethically. People came out of their classes not as stage hypnotists for entertainment value but as clinical hypnotherapists for the benefit of other people; to help them mentally, emotionally and physically. I have also realised how close is the link between meditation and hypnosis and how well the healing and hypnosis works together.

Alternative therapies are extremely diverse and to do them well takes many years of study. There are many aspects that are of interest to me, acupuncture, homeopathy, aromatherapy, Indian head massage, reflexology, the study of herbs and their uses and the list goes on. They all have their place in the healing of a person; healing the whole body and they all are involved with the giving of oneself.

I believe that courses of learning are essential to everyone's personal development; they are always of benefit, as learning of any description is never wasted. I had never gone on courses before; I didn't believe in them, I used to always think that I would learn by what I was feeling, by what was in my heart, I did not want to listen to authoritarian bodies telling me what to do, I wanted to do it my way.

The first course that I ever enrolled on made me realise the value of the experience of others; it was a counselling course. For the first five minutes we had to look at the blackboard and the subject that was covered was discipline. I remember reading what the tutor had written and shaking my head. He asked me what I was thinking and I told him that it had taken me twenty years to learn those lessons and here was somebody telling me the answers in five minutes.

It made me realise that other people have knowledge of things that I do not and that I could benefit from the experience of others and that moment changed my whole view of the learning process. My tutor was a man called Larry Manden, who was born in Germany. His father was a politician; a Jewish politician who was murdered during the war. Larry and his brother and sister were taken to a concentration camp and the rest I am sure you can imagine. His wife Sally was a yoga teacher and an extremely proficient one; she was born in India and was a very spiritual lady. I observed her classes for about eighteen months and was very impressed; Yoga helps so much with strength and flexibility, combining the harmony of mind and body.

Going back to Larry's childhood, the children, by means unknown, managed to get free and came over to England, where their sister was later adopted and went to live in

America. The two boys were fostered by a famous actor and would be picked up from school in a Rolls Royce, which must have been pretty special for them. They were eventually passed from home to home and had a lot of difficulties as young children with so much to overcome. Goodness knows how the mind of a child copes with such things but children, as we know are thankfully very resilient, which is just as well with all the inhumanity and thoughtlessness of adults. I know that the whole family were re-united not very long ago; their mother now living in Israel. I think that it was too late for the family to live together again, too many years had passed and they all had created their own lives.

What an achievement for Larry to teach counselling. He had worked through all the hurt and pain that he had gone through and is out there helping others. I have a great deal of respect for that and he taught me so much that I may help others and his discipline is now an inherent part of my life. It was an important lesson to learn that there are so many people out there with so much to give. In every field of learning there is someone, who knows more than you. Someone who can teach you more and mankind can only benefit from continuous learning.

All these people are working for Spirit in their own ways, with their own inspirations. We get news of people all the time, who have done things wrong; done bad things, so it is really good to know that there are millions of people out there who are working for the good of humanity, to make the world a better place. I have met so many of them and it gladdens my heart and I thank all of the people, who have taught me their skills.

I acquired a Masters Certificate in Hypnotherapy, Diplomas in Counselling Skills, and Skills in Families Matter; working with group therapy and working with children. All these things helped me to be a little bit wiser and to realise all the crises that we go through in life; crises of the youngest child, the middle child, the eldest child. Crises of divorce, loss of our parents, step-parenting and the terrible crises of abuse, physical and emotional.

Today I spend a lot of my time helping young people with life skills and I do this through the YMCA. We have a place in Doncaster called the Roger Worth training centre, which is designed to specifically help young people to find accommodation and to put their lives in order. We use different techniques to help them to understand themselves and their problems. Sometimes it is a lecture or demonstration, sometimes role-play, sometimes counselling. The majority of these youngsters have been turned out of their homes, rejected by their parents or carers.

Organisations like the YMCA take the kids on and pay them about forty pounds a week, which is about seventy dollars but of course there are conditions attached to this. They must attend lessons on life skills and are helped to find accommodation to give them independence and stability in their lives. They are not yet adults but have passed over the childhood stage and the problem is that they have no money or support at home and often turn to crime simply to survive. Most of them are full of hurt and anger; they hurt from not being loved and cared for. Some of them have been abused; it may have been a father or an uncle, and some of them have had to turn to prostitution to survive.

The project helps to teach the kids that there are people who care; there are good people and good ways to live in the world. It is a very hard and uphill struggle to change their beliefs, as they have been subjected to all sorts of abuse for all of their young lives and now think that this is normal. Lots of people in society reject these kids instead of helping them. They are never offered a chance; people simply assume that they are bad. They only know what life has taught them.

People who abuse children make me so angry; they pretend that it is love but it is NEVER about love. Do they realise the far- reaching damage that they cause to the children? At some point the child will grow up and realise what has been done to them and this will then trigger all the feelings of hurt, anger and confusion. The child often feels guilty, thinking that it is to blame and another young person's life is ruined.

If anyone is reading this book and is committing abuse towards a child, please, please stop now. The things that you are doing are too bad for words. IT IS NOT LOVE, IT IS NEVER ABOUT LOVE and is so very, very damaging to the child. You must also be aware that the abuse may not be physical. If you are constantly shouting and swearing or putting the child down with your words, this is also abuse. I try to tell the young people that I lecture that abuse is always wrong; it is very important for them to realise that the cycle must be broken and that they in turn must not become the abusers. I try to tell them about life and teach them life skills. They need help to turn their lives around and to see that life can offer good things.

I sometimes wonder why life skills are not taught as part of the curriculum in schools. Maybe they are in America but I do not believe that in England our children are taught enough about looking after their well-being. They are taught skills about looking after their bodies physically but not emotionally. Our emotional health is hidden yet of paramount importance to the quality of our lives. We need to also teach the children about all the crises in life that they may encounter. Teach every child, and teach them how to handle things; they need to be prepared because life throws us into many lions' dens.

Sometimes when I am speaking, I see one of the kids with their head down, looking at the floor and I know that I have hit a nerve; they are probably going through the exact crisis that I am speaking about. If they do not get the proper counselling then they go down a treacherous path. They make mistake after mistake, until their lives become a blur of fear and mistrust. Their lives consist of drug abuse, violence, and stealing and even prostitution. They are in dire need of a strong willed, assertive but caring figurehead to take them back to the right way. It is not easy but it is worthwhile. It is important that we understand these youngsters and that we do not look down on them because our own circumstances have been more privileged.

Children are brought up in a myriad of circumstances; some are fortunate, some are not. All are in need of protection and love and certainly not scorn. There are children with single parents; some may not have any money but are loved beyond measure and some stepfamilies blend together admirably. Then there is the other side of the coin; divorce after divorce, stepparents that are cruel and indifferent towards the youngsters. It is bad enough to lose a parent without suffering at the hands of a stranger. All the time that this is happening the child is becoming more and more confused; more fearful and mistrusting of adults and the world becomes a dark place.

It is not enough to teach literacy and mathematics in our schools; we need highly trained counsellors in all of the schools. We need open, approachable people that the children can turn to in absolute confidence, when they need help. This is not a luxury it is a necessity but these people must go through stringent vetting procedures, so that the situation never arises where they add to the suffering. I know that we are gradually moving towards this but in England we desperately need the Children's Commissioner to push this forward. We need someone to oversee all of the Children's Services and their functions; making sure that Social Services and all other governing bodies are working efficiently and effectively for the children.

Abuse of our innocents has been happening for hundreds of years; the scarring of our children. We have more and more mothers and fathers, who are drug abusers; we need to take a zero tolerance approach to this in order to protect our future generations. We first of all have to help all of these people, who have gone down the road of drugs and then the poor unfortunate children, whose lives it has ruined. Surely we have evolved enough to put a stop to this; it is fundamental to our society to stop it.

All children need to be taught life skills, so that the abused do not become the abusers. If we can counsel the abused to make them respect themselves again, they will then respect society and their own families. If any of the readers feel that they have something to offer in this work, please search for a good counselling course. They are usually very reasonable, so that most people can afford to do them. If you do not have the money, then maybe you can go on a course that is funded. The effort of searching one out is worth it, as you will learn so much.

I believe that everyone should do a counselling course at some time in their life. This could be another part of the school curriculum; we would learn about ourselves and understand others so much more. Do as many courses as you can within your lifetime, for the strong must endeavour to help the weak and the vulnerable.

There are so many people out there, who are doing wonderful jobs; jobs that benefit humanity. You could choose to be one of them. I thank God for all the teachers it has been my pleasure to meet. I encourage all the youngsters to go on the courses; to learn to do things properly and to gain the knowledge. Never, ever lose the thirst for knowledge and let God be your inspiration. Learn something new every day, for we can learn from everything and everybody.

Once you have got the knowledge, in whatever subject, use it wisely; use the knowledge for the good of others. If you are young and feeling lost and lacking in direction, try to get yourself on a course. Do whatever you are interested in and do not be afraid that your friends will laugh at you or that they have no interest in your subject. This does not matter do it for you. You may be the teacher of tomorrow, who helps someone your age along his or her path. Never think that you are less of a person than someone else and never think that you do not deserve to learn or to better your life. Go forward my friend, always forward, and may God walk with you every step of the way.

Post Natal Depression

Sandra is a young woman in her late twenties; she is tall and slim with long, blonde hair. When Sandra gave birth to her first baby, she suffered extremely bad post-natal depression. It was so bad that during her second pregnancy the obstetrician placed her under the care of the consultant psychiatrist. He was to monitor her progress after the birth. She gave birth to a boy, Nathan, and both came through the labour absolutely fine and throughout the pregnancy and the labour Sandra was very well. Nathan was a golden baby and was no trouble at all; he slept a lot and cried very little. All was going wonderfully well until three weeks after the birth, when the depression hit again.

The psychiatrist that she saw prescribed Valium, 15-20 mg, per day but things did not get any better and Sandra felt that she was in a huge, black hole that she could not get out of. She became so desperately ill that she overdosed; taking thirty-two tablets and her mum in desperation rang me. Her mum is the aunt of Karen; a girl that I had been treating for cancer and Karen gave her my number. My clinic was fully booked that day but her voice sounded so desperate, that I agreed to stay on and to wait for her.

The first session that she came she simply cried and cried as she poured out her story. I listened throughout the sobs to her story and told her to lie on the couch. After the healing she seemed very relaxed and calm and told me that she had experienced a wonderful sense of peace and she tried to describe the feeling to me. I could see the spirit of Sandra's grandmother was with her all of the time. Sandra went home that day and halved her medication. I was not so sure that this was a sensible thing to do, as anyone knows, who has taken this drug, it is very powerful and takes virtually years to be weaned off it. Her psychiatrist was shocked and necessarily cautious. He agreed to prescribe a drug called Carbemazepine, which Sandra informed me, was an anti-depressant booster. He could not give her this before, as she was taking too much of the Valium.

She saw me again for treatment one week later and contrary to my advice, saying that she was feeling well, she dropped the Valium to three milligrams and suffered no apparent side effects. After the next visit she stopped the Valium altogether. This worried me and I cautioned her strongly against doing this without first consulting her psychiatrist but she was adamant that she felt fine. She made an appointment to explain things to her own doctor and the consultant psychiatrist, telling them that she had sought help from alternative therapy and told them that she was now off the Valium altogether and feeling much better and was able to cope.

I must stress here that I would never advise anyone to go against the advice of the medical profession; this is highly dangerous, especially in the case of depression. Both the doctors asked Sandra for my card saying that they must speak to me. The psychiatrist told her to continue with the Carbamazepine for the time being but to contact him immediately should there be any changes. I spoke to the doctors regarding my concerns and stated that I advised Sandra to continue with her medication until told otherwise by her doctor. Sandra went on from strength to strength without the tablets and is now back at work full-time and coping well with her two children. She sees me now once a fortnight for her 'treat' and says that she will always do so.

Sean vs Leuk:
The Final Battle

Linda, the lady who specialises in reflexology in my clinic, came to me one day to say that her friend's son was extremely ill. He was fifteen years old and had leukaemia and it had returned for the third time. I told her to bring him along for us to look at him and that we would do everything that we possibly could. We treated Sean for quite a long time; giving him everything that we had at our disposal. I won't tell you any more of the story, as Sean has printed a letter, telling it in his own words, he called it 'The Final Battle.'

The Final Battle

26th June 2001

I was bored and I could not be bothered to move or do anything. I was so depressed with life and what it had given me. Being told that I had cancer for the third time in the fifteen years of my life left me with no mental confidence or self-belief.

What was the point in trying to fight it? It keeps coming back to haunt, tease and torment me and after six weeks of lying in a hospital bed, wired up like a laboratory rat, staring at the same four walls. I did not feel like doing a lot.

I watched TV for two weeks, until I was told by friends to visit a man named Mick.

As I walked into the little building I was met by a laid back, calmly collected man. We walked into a little back room, where he told me to lay down on a table in the middle of the room. Mick told me to close my eyes and to concentrate on the words that he was saying. He talked about a great battle, The Final Battle.

It was between Leuk and me; it was a battle in which I was dressed in fine armour. I was holding my mighty sword; Excalibur and we would kill Leuk once and for all.

As Mick talked, he told me to be confident and he taught me to believe that I can and WILL destroy Leuk forever. This new found confidence and self-belief helped me to keep fighting no matter what life throws at me. I got the last results back from the tests that I had done, all pointing to the all clear; the leukaemia had gone from my system.

I believe that Mick had a lot to do with this, so I thank him greatly for my life.

By Sean Towers (aged 15)

Footnote:
On the day that my wife went into hospital, Sean sent my assistant Linda a text message to her mobile phone. It said 'Leuk is dead'.

She says that she will never erase it.

God Bless you Sean, you are a fighting champion.

Doncaster Operatic Society:

Memoires

I mentioned before that I love to perform on the stage and have been involved in quite a few productions in Doncaster. I was the lion in the Wizard of Oz and have also appeared in Oliver, Annie, Oklahoma and many more. It has been my pleasure to work with some lovely, talented young people over the years. Some of them were very confident and others not so confident. I became friendly with a particularly nice young man called Thomas while performing in Annie and Oliver and he sent me this letter that I would like to share with you.

Dear Mick,

You may not remember me but I thought that I ought to write to you, as it has been a while since I have seen you. I'm Thomas, who played the Tin Man in The Wizard of Oz, and worked with you in Annie and before that Oliver, with the Doncaster Operatic Society.

I haven't gone in for Oklahoma this year, as I had to concentrate on my GCSE's and I am not sure when I will return to the company. I hear that you too have decided not to be in the show, so that you can be with your wife. I hope that she is soon better and I thought that I would write to see how you both are.

I also wanted to tell you that I wrote about you in my GCSE English exam (well you wanted to be in my memoirs didn't you, so this is the first step). The question asked me to do a piece of extended writing about someone, who has made a difference to my life and how someone has been important to me. I told them about how we worked together on many shows and how you helped me and everyone else, when we had a problem. How you created a good atmosphere in the dressing room, whenever there was a crisis and how of course you always inspired and encouraged me to carry on acting, by having faith in my being able to make it to the top.

I do hope that I make it someday. If I do, I will most certainly include you in my memoirs. I thought that it would be nice to let you know that I put you in my exam writing. This is basically just to check that you and your wife are okay and to make sure that you do not forget me. Obviously I hope that we work together again soon but until then look after each other and have happy times.

Yours sincerely,
Thomas Howes

From Mick:
Thank you for your letter and kind thoughts Thomas and for mentioning me in your exam. I have now put you down in my memoirs, so I will certainly not forget you. Carry on to the top and God Bless.

Wings to Fly

This is the story of a young girl, who entered my clinic just over three years ago.

She is the mother of a small child and was currently being treated at the hospital for terminal cancer. A very brave and determined young woman; she had fought it time after time, only for it to return again. Her situation had reached a critical stage when she came to the clinic for treatment.

She heard that a book was being written about the healing that has been done over the years and asked if she may add her own contribution. Her own story in her own words.

Karen's story:

I met Mick in August 2001. I came to him a broken person; I left with wings to fly...

In May 1997, age 28 and with a five-month-old baby, I was diagnosed with breast cancer.

Six years earlier, I had a fibroid adenoma (a benign tumour) removed. My reaction? I laughed. Not the laugh of someone enjoying a hysterical comedy, but the one of someone in shock and disbelief. I suppose how you would laugh if you had won the lottery, only I had not won the lottery, but had been dealt a losing hand in a poker game at Bellargios. The chips were truly down.

After a mastectomy, auxiliary lymph node clearance on one side, eight months of chemotherapy and six weeks of radiotherapy, my life gradually got back to normal (I have deliberately not mentioned which side my mastectomy was done on. Why? Because my prosthesis is so good that you cannot tell; plus you have a 50/50 chance of being right if you guess).

In August 2000, I started to have an ache in my left side and my back hurt. It is very easy, once you have had cancer, to think that every cough and ache is the cancer coming back. With every new symptom that I had, I always gave it at least two weeks before I mentioned anything to the doctor.

During those two weeks, I tried to remember if I could have done anything to cause the ache/pain. Usually, after a couple of weeks, the pain would be gone. This time however, it did not.

I mentioned it to my doctor at my next check up and he said that we would wait a few weeks more to see if it resolved itself. Those weeks passed and I still had the back pain and the pain in my side. The next time that he saw me he arranged for a bone scan and a liver ultrasound scan. In all, it took ten weeks, from first getting the pain, to getting the results of the tests. The cancer had returned and had now spread to my liver and bones. My best friend and my soulmate, Louise, came with me to get the results.

In a way, I should have realised that it would not be good news as my appointment was at the end of the day (I presume so that when I was hysterical, the other patients would not hear and be upset). Sue, who had been my Breast Care nurse, just said a nervous 'hello' to me when she saw me in the waiting room and normally she would come over to chat.

She later told me that she did not come over in case I asked her the results, which I would not have done. The consultant walked in and sat down beside me. He uttered the most destructive sentence that I have ever heard. 'There is no easy way to tell you this...'

I cannot begin to put into words, the utter disbelief and despair that I felt. Here I was, thirty-one years old, separated from my husband, with a three-and-a-half-year-old boy, and my world just blown apart. It was bad enough when I got cancer the first time, but everything had been going so well. I had now had three years of good quality life and it had come back. The doctor then said, 'The most that we can give you is two years.' 'Two years?' I said, 'I don't want two years, I want twenty, I want the rest of my life. What about Joel, my son?'

The rest of what he said passed in a blur. I will never forget the date; it was October 31st. It was Halloween Night, and for the first time, I had told Joel that I would take him 'trick or treating.'

I can't remember who was looking after Joel whilst I was at the hospital, probably my parents.

After telling them the news, I made them go home and then, and I will never know how we did it, but Louise and I got Joel dressed and took him 'trick or treating,' while trying to act as if everything was normal. In some ways it was a good distraction and a delay from having to deal with reality.

I remember that at some point in the evening, we went to the off-licence and bought a bottle of Southern Comfort and a bottle of lemonade, intending to drink to numb the reality. My parents had rung my ex-husband and the three of us, Louise, Alan and me, sat on the settee in mortified silence. As it happened, I only had a sip of the alcohol, but I think that even if I had drunk the entire bottle neat, I would have remained woefully sober. So, on the 31st October 2000, I began a truly horrendous emotional roller coaster, that would eventually lead me to Mick.

The consultant who gave me the news referred me to an Oncology Professor at Weston Park Hospital. Up until this point I had been treated at Doncaster, which has a cancer unit, but Weston Park is solely an Oncology Hospital. It was there that I met Professor Coleman. He told me that I could have chemotherapy, but there was only a one in three chance that it would work and at first I refused. When I first lost my hair, my son Joel was only seven months old, so he was blissfully unaware of what was happening but now he was a curious three-and-a-half-year-old. How could I explain it? What would I tell him?

Being a nurse and having nursed patients with cancer I knew what to expect. Believe me, in this instance, a little knowledge is a dangerous thing, oh to have been blissfully ignorant. Anyway, my main concern was that Joel's last memories of me would be a bald mummy who was always being sick. I just did not want that for him, but then my dad said, 'I'm sure that Joel would rather have a bald mummy than no mummy at all.' If you knew my dad, then you would know that he is not one to show his emotions, so when he said that I realised that I had to give it a try, for Joel and for him.

After much deliberation and thought, I decided to tell Joel that mummy was poorly with something called cancer. I took the decision to name it because I thought that otherwise he would think that everyone who was poorly had cancer.

I told him that I was going to have some medicine to help with the pain, I never said 'to make me better' as I wanted to be truthful to him but without scaring him. Amazingly the chemotherapy worked. One minute I was being told that the cancer had returned and that I had just a one in three chance of survival, and therefore preparing for my possible death and the next I was being told that the treatment had been successful.

In March 2001, I had to have a right, total hip replacement. The cancer had eaten away at my bone to such an extent, had I fallen, the bone would have crumbled and I would have been in a mess. So that was another hurdle to overcome.

I spent three months rehabilitating, all the while wondering if I would have the time to enjoy my new hip before I became ill again.

I am a bit unsure of the exact dates, but during mid 2001, tumours were found in my brain and both eyes. It seemed that every time I overcame one hurdle, another was slapped down in front of me. It was an emotional roller-coaster, where one minute you are being told that you are going to die, the next that the treatment had worked and the next that they had found it somewhere else on your body. The stress became too much and that is when I found Mick McGuire.

I found out about him through my aunty, who was being treated successfully by Mick for a back problem. She mentioned that he did healing and although I had always been a strong and positive person, in August 2001, I was a broken woman. I could not deal with the extreme changes in my illness anymore. More than anything, I went to Mick to restore my sanity and my fighting spirit so that I could continue my battle.

I remember that during the first couple of sessions all I did was cry. Mick gave me healing, but I just lay there, shaking with emotion. After the first time that I saw Mick, he said that he would give me healing for free. I was astounded, as I had not expected this; my family were prepared to pay, no matter what the cost.

On many an occasion I would offer to pay, but Mick always refused. I tried to make it up a little by buying biscuits, cakes and presents at Christmas. When I have told people that Mick helped me for free, they said that this was the sign of a true healer. He wanted to heal for healing's sake, rather than monetary gain.

Mick got me to open up about how I was feeling and it was good to offload to a stranger. Sometimes, there were things that I wanted to say, but could not say to my family or friends as it would have had them in tears. I would then have had to be strong for them and put what I was feeling to one side. So spilling all to Mick was good, it meant that I could say exactly how the battle with cancer was making me feel, without having to worry or feel guilty that I was upsetting anyone.

I told Mick that the thought of leaving my son was unbearable. My dream was to watch him play football on a winter's Sunday morning while I shivered on the sidelines. I have always been open to alternative therapies and found the world of Spirit that Mick told me about fascinating.

When he gave me healing, I could feel the heat and energy coming from his hands. They would start off at normal temperature but by the end of the session, would be boiling hot. Sometimes, after a healing, he would say, 'That was peaceful.'

To help me to battle the cancer, Mick gave me various treatments, reflexology and hypnotherapy as well as the healing. During the hypnotherapy he would ask me to imagine somewhere peaceful and serene where I could relax. I am a firm believer that stress is a strong negative factor in cancer. He helped me to use visualisation exercises, where the cancer was an evil black knight.

I had an army of silver soldiers whom I had to command to attack this evil knight and drive it out of my body. I used to do this visualisation mainly at night, so that it was my last thought before I went to sleep. Hopefully then, the thoughts of the silver army attacking the black knight would carry on working in my subconscious while I slept.

Before each session of healing began, Mick would take the time to ask me how I had been since the last session. At the end of each session he would always ask if I had felt anything during the healing. Often he would have at least one other person in the room, and they would also join in the healing. Sometimes I would be aware of a chill down one side of me, from the person on that side giving me healing. When the healing had ended, Mick would talk about how he had received messages and guidance from the spirit world as he healed me.

As I mentioned earlier, I had cancer in my brain. Approximately four months after receiving radiotherapy to the affected areas, I was given a brain scan to see if the tumours had responded to the treatment.

Unbeknown to me, Mick had spoken to Spirit on an earlier occasion. He had basically said that if I were allowed to die, then he would never heal again. For a man who is so passionate about his healing, and with as many success stories behind him, it was quite a profound statement to make. When I did get the news of the scan, it showed that the tumours had gone into remission and there were many tears as I broke the news. Then Mick surprised me with his own revelation. Spirit had told him that the miracle that he wanted for the young woman would be given.

He had known before me, that the scan results would be good, but he had not told me until I had the scientific proof. It is now six years since I was first diagnosed with cancer. During that time, I think that I have astounded the medical profession.

I have had cancer in my breast, lymph nodes, eyes, brain, liver and bones and yet I am alive today, looking and feeling so well, that if you met me and heard my story, you would think that I had a most vivid imagination.

I am the living proof that the black knight can be crushed, but without Mick and the help of his team, I doubt that I would be here. Instead I would have died a defeated, demoralised wreck. Thank you Mick, for giving me wings to fly again.

N.B.
Sadly Karen has now passed over to the spirit world, but her life was thankfully extended a little that she had more time with her son. Our thoughts and prayers go out to him and her family. She gave permission before her passing for this story to be published in this book. God bless you darling.

Positive Thoughts: A Chance to Redeem

To heal is the most beautiful gift of all, to help people who are suffering pain; be it physical, mental or emotional and to bring peace to the mind and comfort to the body. These are wonderful gifts from Spirit, from God.

I believe that each and any one of us has the ability to heal and just as we have great artists, we also have people who can sketch or copy, but everyone can paint a picture. So it is with healing, everyone can do it. Some are greater healers than others but all are capable. To heal is to give of love, as a mother does to her baby child; the cuddles and closeness heal the spirit of the child and send forth love. Some people use healing words, they comfort others by what they say and it is usually a natural thing to them.

Today on our television screens there are more and more programmes about psychics, clairvoyants and mediums and they are shown demonstrating their wonderful gifts and yet there are no programmes about healers. To me out of all the gifts that I am blessed to have; to heal is the greatest gift of all.

When I first went to the churches and was told that I was a healer; that I had healing hands; well this confused me. I thought that to be a healer you had to be someone better than myself; I thought that you had to be somebody really special; maybe a vicar or a priest. I thought that you needed to be working for God and thought that it could not be true that an ordinary man or woman could have the healing gift. It was a wonderful thought that they gave me that day and I could not have left it; I had to follow it up. Spirit most certainly directed me to the church.

I believe that it came at the time that I was beginning to lose my faith in God. During my years in the Army, because I was Catholic, I spent some time with some Catholic priests in Cologne and was taught about taking confession and different aspects of the Catholic faith. I listened intently to the stories that the priests would tell about their time during the war. One priest had been on death row, speaking to the people who were about to be executed. I often wondered whether it was the right thing to do; to execute people who had committed murder. To finish their life here on Earth, so that they can do no more harm. One part of me said that this was the safe thing to do; however it is a huge thing for the human race to take upon itself.

The rest of the course of my life was to direct me towards Spiritualism, from where I have learned so much of the spirit realms. I can tell you that since I have known of the spirit realms they have taught me that we must not do this. We must not kill these people who have murdered, as the spirit realms do not want them. They tell me that they do not want these people; people who have committed murder and hideous crimes. They tell me that they should be kept here in our earthly kingdom and must have the opportunity to redeem their souls. They must do work that will offset some of the horrendous deeds that they have committed and they must have the chance to learn remorse in order that the spirit world is not filled with dark and damaged souls; for the spirit world is a place of the greatest love and light. These people need to work for love before they pass over.

Maybe they could work with animals or do things for charity; maybe they could paint pictures or write stories. When they have committed horrendous crimes, they must dedicate their entire lives to doing good, to offset what they have done. Spirit said that this would offset their crimes. They said that they must not be sent over, until their souls have had the chance to do good work on the material plane.

They will not be able to progress in the spirit world, until all the people, whom they have done terrible things to, forgive them and this may never happen. Sometimes they do not even reach the spirit world but remain in the darkness. When they pass over, because of what they have done, they may bury their souls deep in pits of darkness and may never be rescued from these places.

Their chance to redeem themselves is on this plane, where others could later stand and say that they had finally done some good. Even if they are locked up for the rest of their lives; which would have to be the case for some people, they could write, paint, do work for charities, some may even pray or read the Bible. Maybe they will find God in their darkness and feel remorse within themselves for their deed.

The majority of people throughout our lives try to do for good rather than for evil; we try to help people rather than hurt them, to love rather than to hate. We can go which way we want, because we have free will and it is our choice. If we take a life for a life, are we then acting as God?

Some people think that it states in the Bible an eye for an eye but it actually says that you shall not take an eye for an eye but turn the other cheek.

Of course we have the right as a society to stop murders being committed and to punish these people and to keep them locked safely away, where they can do no harm. This is pure common sense, we do not want murderers let loose among our children and families.

To kill them is entirely different; to send them to the spirit world where they can spend maybe thousands of years in the darkness, for they cannot move on until they find forgiveness. There is a natural law and it is a spiritual law and it is the same for everyone, good or bad, even for people who are in prisons; people who have robbed, injured or murdered others. Whatever we sow we will reap. You cannot escape your punishment in the spirit world; everything throughout your life is recorded and all the bad things that you have done will be brought before you. Your own soul will be your own judge and jury and believe me no one is harsher.

Another very important thing that we must all do is to sow good thoughts. Do not send out bad thoughts to anyone or anything; always send out thoughts of peace, thoughts of love and harmony. If you feel bitter and twisted and you send out bad thoughts to someone, you will reap those bad thoughts; they will come directly back to you with more force than they were sent.

If you try to have good thoughts to your fellow brothers and sisters, you will reap all those back too. If they have hurt you, do not send vengeful thoughts out to them; send them love and light and pray that they will see the error of their ways. These loving thoughts will return to you tenfold.

If your fellow man has been nasty or hurtful to you, do not plot revenge. You are then going down the same path as them and you must be above this. Keep your soul loving and light and surround yourself and your aura with love and peace. Never surround yourself with dark thoughts, as like attract like and you will draw more negativity towards yourself.

There is a Universal Law; it is a spiritual law and it is God's law. This governs everything that we do, say and think and it applies to everybody. What we give out will return to us and when we have done or said something wrong, we know how guilty we feel. Try your best to err on the side of God.

There are so many people in this life, who have had horrific things happen to them. Some have had their children killed, their loved ones killed by bombs. Our Earth suffers disaster after disaster. Our life here on the material plane is so short and it is so difficult. We all have many obstacles to overcome. The Earth plane is our school; it is where we come to learn. We need to learn all about our emotions, to understand everything that we think and feel and ourselves. We are here to overcome these lessons; to teach our spirits to be the best that they can be.

We know, when we love somebody, how good it feels. Ask a mother holding her newly born, how big her heart feels, it is enormous and saturated with love. What a wonderful feeling. How much better is this than the feelings of guilt and hatred? When we are troubled and twisted inside, sending out bad thoughts; how this drags us down mentally and physically.

The bad thoughts that go out into the world keep all the negativity and grief circling around. They are out there in the atmosphere, waiting to be picked up and acted upon.

Endeavour to keep your thoughts positive and loving all the time. I know that we all feel anger and rage at some time but once it is over let it go; do not keep it going around and around as it will only cause harm.

We need to lock the people who have done really bad things away from society, but we must give them a chance to redeem themselves and to work for mankind. There are all sorts of ways to do this without putting anyone at risk.

I know that it is a huge thing to think about but Spirit tells us that this is the right thing to do. These people need to stand before Spirit that someone can say for them, 'This person is sorry for the wrong that they have done; they are sorry for the hurt that they have caused.' They need to stand with remorse and have one single person to say that they have done some good.

The deeds that they do can live with the victims' families for a lifetime and the perpetrators must be committed to working for forgiveness. They must be given the chance to work for forgiveness for the rest of their lives, so that when it comes to the time when they will judge themselves, they will be able to say with a true heart, 'I did wrong, but I am so very, very sorry.' There is an inbred thing in each of us that says we should not hurt, we should not kill. These are God's laws and we know that we are doing wrong, when we go against His will.

When we finally pass to Spirit, judge and jury do not judge us, we judge ourselves, and for each one of us knows better than anyone else everything that we have said and done here on Earth and everything that we have thought.

We judge ourselves more harshly than anyone else ever could, because we are the one person who knows everything about ourselves. We may be able to deceive other people here on Earth; deceive people that we love, even deceive the Police but the one person that we can never deceive is ourselves. We are aware of every thought, word and deed and one day we will have to face that. How will we judge ourselves on that day? How do you judge yourself this day?

What have you learned here on this Earth? We will judge ourselves by the law that governs all people and we will set our own punishments. There are many important issues that concern the human race that we must think seriously about, euthanasia and the death penalty. So often we live in a world of hate, where people kill for all sorts of reasons or religious indoctrinations. The suicide bombers, who kill and are prepared to give up their own lives, may believe that they kill in the name of God. God is the ultimate source of love.

There are wars and battles of power; the killing of the soldiers and the innocents; the murders of vulnerable women and children. We live in a world of terrorists, robbers and muggers. Today seems to be the world of the drug addict, the drug dealers.

Their God is the same God as our God. He taught us that we shall not kill; not for any reason but one day they will judge themselves and their deeds.

Spirit gave me a very strong message that we must not kill these people and send them over; the spirit world does not want them in their state of darkness. They must first pay their dues here on Earth; they must have the time to be remorseful and work to balance the wrong that they have done. Food for thought my friend.

Easter 2002

I remember this date vividly as it was to hold a shocking revelation that would turn my world upside down; it was to be the greatest trial ever regarding my faith and spirit.

The healings in the clinic were going very well, I was working long hours in the Sanctuary but was also working hard during rehearsals for the production of the stage show Oklahoma. I have performed on the stage in Doncaster for a lot of years now and find this to be a pastime that I can be totally absorbed in and it helps me to forget about everything else.

Because of my busy work schedule, I was beginning to feel really tired and felt that I needed a break. I have a caravan, or mobile home, as some people call them, in the coastal resort of Bridlington, which is on the East coast of England. I thought that Dorothy and I would go for the weekend for a rest. I finished work on the Friday teatime and looked forward to our weekend away. We did a little bit of shopping to take with us and then packed up the car and away we went. We had a lovely drive down there and Dorothy nodded off during the journey. I noticed that she had been looking a little tired of late; I think it is because she looks after our grandchildren all the time. They sometimes stay overnight and I keep telling her that she has them too much, but she won't listen to me. She adores them and loves them to be with us.

This was a weekend away on our own; it was to enable us to re-charge our batteries. We both slept very well on the Friday evening and had a nice leisurely breakfast on the Saturday morning; bacon, sausage eggs and tomatoes with a nice cup of coffee to set us off for the day. We went into Bridlington as we usually do; we always follow the same routine, Dorothy goes off shopping, which she loves, and I go to the local betting office for a bet on the horses. Dorothy then brings her shopping to me and we go for a nice lunch in one of the cafes or restaurants.

That particular day however Dorothy came back to the betting office within twenty minutes. She said that she was not feeling very well at all and said that her stomach was swollen and painful. I thought that maybe she had a touch of indigestion from the breakfast and told her to sit herself down on the chair for a little while but she remarked that she was still feeling no better.

We decided to go and have a light lunch to see if this would settle things down but she couldn't eat anything and still seemed in a lot of discomfort. I had to take this seriously as my wife is never ill and is not one to complain about little things. I finally decided that we would go back home, even though we had looked forward to the break; I felt that she did not look well enough to stay.

By teatime we were on our way back and Dorothy booked in to see the doctor on the following Monday morning. She went along with her sister and the doctor told her that maybe it was a cyst. Dorothy likes her sister to accompany her for things that she terms 'ladies' problems. The doctor said that he would send her to the hospital for further checks. I wasn't concerned at this point, and I thought that it would turn out to be something simple.

The telephone rang in my clinic and the girls called me urgently out of the treatment room and it was then that my wife told me that the doctor was ninety-nine per cent certain that she had cancer. Her voice was trembling and she was crying. I grabbed my hat and coat and left work immediately to go home; the girls cancelled all of my appointments.

We have gone through many things together, as people do who have been married for a long time but this was something entirely different; it was an enormous trial and test for us to face. I questioned my psychic abilities too; I have seen illness in people many times when I have been healing them, so why had I not seen this coming in my wife?

They requested that she attended the hospital for more in depth investigations. Dorothy has a phobia regarding needles and injections and of course needed quite a few blood tests. She also needed an M.R.I. scan and she suffers from claustrophobia. I decided that I would use my hypnotherapy training to help her with this. I hypnotised her to cope with any injections and gave her some hypnotherapy and visualisation to cope with the scan.

My team at the clinic threw everything at her that we were capable of doing. Lots and lots of healing, reflexology, Indian head massage, everything. She went through all the preliminary investigations at the hospital wonderfully and she did so very well and finally the time came to speak to the consultant specialist regarding their findings.

His name was Mr. Heslip and we had an appointment to see him on the Friday morning. I hypnotised my wife once again, before we went to the hospital to enable her to cope with whatever diagnosis that she was given. The specialist told my wife that she had a large tumour on her right ovary, which had also spread into the pelvis and peritoneum. She just sat there quietly and simply accepted the information; it was if someone had told her that she had a common cold.

The consultant said that he would like her to come in to hospital on the following Monday morning for an operation and that he would like her to have the pre-operative checks done immediately, so that she would be ready and he would have all the necessary information with him for the Monday morning.

He also wanted her to speak to the anaesthetist, who would explain all the procedures and answer any questions that she may have. Dorothy nodded in agreement and said that it was okay to do this. The consultant said goodbye and left the room but the nurse who was in attendance came to sit beside us. She asked if we had understood what he had told us. That it was not a cyst but a tumour on the ovary. I said that yes we had fully understood. My wife looked at me and then at the nurse. 'Yes, I have got cancer.' She said it very calmly and controlled.

The nurse commented, 'You seem very calm, Mrs. McGuire.' 'Oh yes, my husband has hypnotised me, I am absolutely fine.' The nurse then checked her blood pressure, which was normal and yet Dorothy has had blood pressure problems for such a long time.

The doctor asked her how she had got up to the ward and she said that she had climbed the stairs. He asked if she felt okay and she laughed and told him that she had to wait for me at the top of the stairs; I had to stop to get my breath back. He told her that she looked extremely well and she said, 'Yes, I am, I'm fine.'

The anaesthetist turned up and explained to my wife the seriousness of the operation. He told her that she would need a full hysterectomy with the removal of the peritoneum and the removal of the cancer from her pelvis. He said that she would need an epidural as well as the anaesthetic and that she would have some distress with her breathing afterwards. He went thoroughly through all the procedures and treatment from start to finish.

Amazingly, when it was all over, my wife was still in a positive frame of mind; she remained very calm and collected. We went to the hospital cafe for a cup of tea and I called to telephone the girls at the clinic to let them know how the consultation had gone. I knew that they would be eagerly waiting at the other end, as they were all deeply concerned about her.

There was another thing on my mind as well, a young boy called Sean, who I had been treating at the clinic for leukaemia; he was getting his results that day and said that he would telephone the clinic to tell me the outcome.

He too had endured all the hospital treatments combined with lots of healing. The girls told me that he was cured; he had telephoned to say that his scan showed no sign of the leukaemia, I felt so elated for him, absolutely jubilant. This young boy was cured.

What a mixed bag of emotions I felt that day, fear for my wife, yet happiness for a patient. It seemed awful to spare a moment to feel happy, when my personal life felt catastrophic. I had given Sean hypnotherapy for his leukaemia. I told him to give himself a black knight to fight Leuk's army. He sent one of the girls a text message that day, which simply said, 'Leuk is dead.' She says that she will never remove it.

Just after six o'clock that evening, we had made all the calls; informed everyone who needed to know and we settled down for a quiet evening in front of the television. We talked about what was to come, about Dorothy going into Weston Park, the Oncology hospital to have the operation, which was to be followed by six sessions of chemotherapy, a daunting prospect for anyone.

There was a knock on the door and it was the cancer specialist, Mr. Heslip, he asked if he might have a word with us. We invited him into the lounge, where my wife greeted him with, 'I hope that you haven't come for any more blood?' 'No, no,' he replied, 'but I think that you should sit down.' This sort of statement immediately raises your heart rate and blood pressure; I wondered what they had found.

He came straight to the point. 'I have cancelled the operation on Monday as there is no evidence of any tumour on your right ovary.' 'Is that a good sign or is it a bad sign?' I asked. 'I have no idea,' he replied, 'but we would like your wife to come in for further tests on Tuesday.' We did not know what to think; were we in the clear or not?

It was a very restless weekend but the Tuesday came and off we went once again and I used the hypnosis to help Dorothy to feel calm. We stayed there all day for the tests and finished late in the afternoon. She was to go back at a later date for the results and the results were that she had primary peritoneum cancer. She also had second or third stage ovarian cancer, which had extended into the pelvis. The cancer readings, which she had, should have been between 33-36, her readings were almost 1200. They decided that they would not operate but would give Dorothy chemotherapy first.
It is strange how we tend to concern ourselves with material things and suddenly, when life is so fragile, they fade into complete insignificance. After three chemotherapy sessions my wife seemed very well, the team had combined two types of the drugs together and it was a very potent cocktail.

Dorothy had the chemotherapy treatments on Fridays and she would be fine on Friday night and all day Saturday but Sunday morning she would start with the pain. The pain was all over her body and she would be poorly maybe for the rest of the week.

On the few days that she felt well, we took advantage and went to the coast for some different scenery and mental upliftment. Dorothy managed to tolerate four of the more aggressive types of chemotherapy but on the fifth time she asked if she might have the easier one.

My team of girls and I continued with the healing and alternative therapies all the way throughout her treatment. She lost her hair and we got a couple of wigs from the hospital, which actually really suited her. Her hair has been thinning for quite a while now, so the false hair looked wonderful. Her attitude was extremely positive and I felt very proud of her. Halfway through the course of treatment I asked the specialist if my wife could be cured and he told me that she could not; all that they could do was to extend her life expectancy. He told me that medicine was progressing all the time but at the moment a cure was not available.

Dorothy attended the hospital for further chemotherapy treatments and remained quite happy and positive. Her hair came back curly and thick, better than I could remember it for years. Her nails were strong and she was back looking after the grandchildren again; her favourite role in life.

The hypnosis worked really well and, although there were many tears, my wife battled with such courage and determination. Unfortunately the cancer returned and my darling wife lost her battle for life in December 2004. My love is with her for eternity.

After thirty years of counselling, thirty years of helping people to handle difficult situations, sometimes to be cured, sometimes to die, to be on the other side, that is very difficult. You have your fears and it is almost impossible sometimes to think in a positive manner. I remember that I asked everybody, who came to the clinic for healing, if they would pray for my wife. I asked all the people in my private circle, I needed to get as many people as possible to pray for her and of course I still pray for her. I am an absolute believer in the power of prayer.

I ask you too dear reader, whether in church or at home or sat in the garden in your quiet moments, please say a prayer for all who are sick; please send them your love and your healing; it is desperately needed in this world of ours.

I thank Spirit for standing by us in our darkest hours, for that doubt, that frailty of the human spirit is always evident during our times of difficulty. I know that God called his daughter back to her heavenly home and that his wisdom is far greater than mine.

The main thing is that whatever happens, whichever way

things have gone, we should always keep faith with God because we need Him even more during the difficult times of our lives. Once again it shows the importance of Prayer, the power of prayer. We prayed so hard for my wife but it is God in His infinite wisdom that decides the outcome. I know that when my day comes I will join her once again and I know until that day she will be around our children and myself. I still have the same utmost faith in God and in the power of Spirit, for no matter what happens they will always be there to help us, to guide us and to lead us. God bless you my darling, your suffering is now over and I know that your journey will continue on the other side. Until we meet again, I love you.

Finale

Finally friends we enter the last chapter of this book. The dictation of this book has been a much more difficult thing to do for me than working in my clinic. I feel confident and at home there, as to serve God is the most simple of things to do. Human beings have a tendency to make even the simplest of tasks difficult, because we are all so full of self-doubt.

When God's calling came to me, I did not feel worthy and thought that he could have chosen someone much better than I to do his work. I know that many of us feel this way in our own particular field of work.

What we must remember is that God loves each and every one of us the same. He has given all of our spirits eternal life and yet so often we make such a mess of it.

The most important thing for us all to realise is there is nothing more important than love; it is the greatest healer of all. If we follow love then we will never go far wrong.

We all have our battles to fight in this life, as did my wife, who battled so courageously with cancer and has now passed over to the world of Spirit. I miss her very much but my faith is as strong as ever. I know that she has gone home, back to the light of God from whence she came. I send all of my love to her in the blessed world of Spirit. I know that she is always around my family watching and helping us with our daily lives. Her love will always be with us, until we meet again in our spiritual home.

I will use the power of prayer and the healing to help me and I have the loving support of my family and friends. I thank Dorothy for all the support and love that she has given to me and the healing work that I do and I dedicate this book to her memory.

I also wish to send out my love and thanks to my dear friend for her devotion in the writing of this book, I know that the spirit world works with her. To my ladies in the clinic I ask for blessings for their dedication to the healing and the comradeship that they bring each day to my place of work.

To our wonderful medium in the Circle of Light, who works so hard for the young people here on Earth, as well as her work for the world of spirit; she is our spiritual teacher and mentor.

I give thanks to God that He placed all of these people upon my path of life, for we never meet anyone by coincidence; it is always meant to be, for whatever reason.

Finally to you dear friends, my brothers and sisters, I want to send to you my heartfelt love and to thank you for taking the time in your busy lives to read this book. I hope that somewhere on these pages you have found something to help you along your path. I know that God will walk with you every step of the way.

Please be strong in whatever is happening in your lives and remember that everything is easier with God's help. Remember that your loved ones never leave you, it only requires a single thought and they are by your side.

Do not be afraid to try the healing my dear friends, to help yourself and the people in your lives, you will be amazed at the outcome. Go onward and forward in everything that you do and leave all that is past behind. Shine your light here on God's beautiful Earth, for the more light that shines the less there is darkness.

God Bless all of you. I love you.